INTERFACT SHAKESPEARE ™

INTERFACT SHAKESPEARE will have you mesmerized in minutes—*and that's a fact!*

◆ **The INTERFACT CD-ROM is packed with games and activities that are challenging, fun, and full of fascinating facts.**

Use the TIME LINE to discover how the plot unfolds.

◆ **Open the book and read *Romeo & Juliet*. You can also discover the historical background of the play and read our version of the story, written in modern English.**

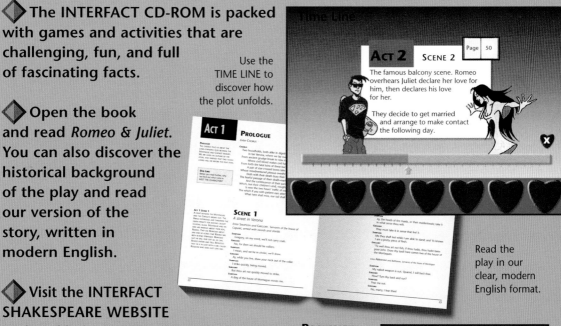

Read the play in our clear, modern English format.

◆ **Visit the INTERFACT SHAKESPEARE WEBSITE and surf links to everything the student of Shakespeare might need to know, including a Homework Helper.**

BOOKMARK

ACT 3	PAGE
SCENE 1	74

DISK LINK
Guess what Shakespeare's more difficult words and phrases mean in the GLOSSARY GAME.

◆ **To get the most out of INTERFACT SHAKESPEARE, use the book, CD-ROM, and website together. Look out for DISK LINKS and BOOKMARKS too. For more information, turn to page 141.**

LOAD UP!
Go to page 139 to find out how to load your CD-ROM and click into action.

WHAT'S ON THE CD-ROM?

HELP SCREEN

Do you need some assistance? Access the Help Screen and learn how to use the disk in no time at all.

Become familiar with the controls and find out how to use:
◇ the games;
◇ the information screens;
◇ the scoring screen.

GLOSSARY GAME

Speak'st thou Shakespearean? Play this game and thou shalt be a merry prattler indeed!

Discover the meaning of many of Shakespeare's most unusual and wonderful words and phrases, and learn some of the English language's most exciting vocabulary.

WALK-THROUGH ROMEO & JULIET

How well do you know the plot? Test your knowledge and learn some more.

Put on your thinking cap and answer a series of multiple-choice questions on *Romeo & Juliet*. The game is full of information which will give you an in-depth understanding of the play.

GIVE HER A KISS

Put your knowledge to the test and help Romeo climb the rope ladder to Juliet's balcony.

It is Romeo and Juliet's wedding night, but they cannot be together until you have answered enough questions correctly. Are you up to the challenge?

ROMEO AND JULIET

THE BOOK, CD-ROM, AND WEBSITE THAT WORK TOGETHER

PRINCETON · LONDON

www.two-canpublishing.com

Two-Can Publishing LLC
234 Nassau Street, Princeton, NJ 08542

Created by

Picthall & Gunzi Ltd
21A Widmore Road, Bromley, Kent BR1 1RW, UK

Consultant: Jane Buckland

BOOK
Story: Barnaby Harward
Editors: Barnaby Harward, Lauren Robertson,
Jill Somerscales, Deborah Murrell, Karen Dolan
Design & Production: Paul Calver
Illustrator: Ray Bryant

CD-ROM
Writers: Barnaby Harward, Deborah Murrell
Editors: Lauren Robertson, Jill Somerscales, Karen Dolan
Illustrator: Ray Bryant
Voices: Mike Evans, Sarah Jones,
Judy Liebert, Christopher Williams

Art Director: Chez Picthall
Editorial Director: Christiane Gunzi

CD-ROM created by
Q&D Multimedia
Producer: Rachel Hall
Programmer: Chris Henson
Sound: Peter Hall
Graphics: Tony Hall

© Two-Can Publishing 2001

"Two-Can," "Interfact," and "Interfact Shakespeare" are trademarks of Two-Can Publishing
Two-Can Publishing is a division of Zenith Entertainment Ltd,
43–45 Dorset Street, London W1U 7NA, UK

For more information on Two-Can books and multimedia, call 1-609-921-6700,
fax 1-609-921-3349, or visit our website at http://www.two-canpublishing.com

ISBN 1-58728-383-2

2 4 6 8 10 9 7 5 3 1

Printed in Hong Kong by Wing King Tong, Hong Kong
Color reproduction by Next Century Ltd, Hong Kong

MAKE A SCENE

Can you remember the characters, props, and sound effects in the most important scenes of the play?

Test your memory of *Romeo & Juliet* in our drag-and-drop game and see if you know who and what you would need if you were directing the key parts of the play.

TIME LINE

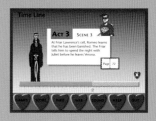

Remind yourself of the storyline with our quick-reference time line.

Romeo & Juliet is a long play, and sometimes it can be difficult to follow the order of the action. Use the Time Line to refresh your memory of the play's most significant events.

WHO SAID WHAT?

Shakespeare's plays are full of famous quotations, but do you know which characters say which ones?

Decide for yourself who you think said which quotation and they will tell you if you're right or wrong. Watch out, though, as some of those characters will really tell you if you get it wrong.

MEET THE CHARACTERS

This introduces all the different characters in the play, from the feuding families to the love-struck couple!

Do you know how many different characters there are in *Romeo & Juliet*? You can find them all here, and discover what part they play in the story.

WHAT'S IN THE BOOK?

What's on the Website?

From the Interfact Shakespeare website you can link to all the best Shakespeare sites on the web. If you're a student or a teacher, or just trying to find out more about the Bard's work, start your research here.

Sites on Shakespeare

From all the links to sites on Shakespeare himself, you can check out Shakespeare titles on the Worldbook site or take a virtual tour of Stratford-upon-Avon with Shakespeare's Birth Place Trust.

Sites on the Globe Theatre

The many sites listed on the Globe Theatre include a link to a map of London in 1600, created by the *Encyclopedia Britannica*, and a performance in a virtual theater when you visit Shakey's Place.

Sites for Students

Shakespeare is made easy here. From the links listed, you can enter the Shakespeare Classroom, the best site on the net for Shakespeare students, or try the Shakespeare Homework Helper and finish that essay.

Sites for Teachers

From the Interfact Shakespeare website teachers can link to, among other things, the complete works of Shakespeare or a site offering advice on the correct pronunciation of Shakespearean English.

PREFACE

by Harold Bloom,
Sterling Professor of the Humanities,
Yale University

It is no surprise that William Shakespeare more than anticipated the phenomenon of multimedia: he invented it. His plays deliberately refuse to stay within the restricted space of the Globe Theatre, since he was at once the most practical and the most imaginative of all dramatists. Motion pictures, television, CD-ROMs, gameplaying, voiceovers, light and sound spectaculars, even virtual reality are all prophesied in the full range of his total production. At his most visionary, in *Macbeth*, *A Midsummer Night's Dream*, *Antony and Cleopatra*, and *The Tempest*, Shakespeare exhausts even our current multimedia resources. He remains an ongoing challenge to fresh developments in the technology of presentation.

Because Shakespeare writes both for the inner and the outer ear, and for the inward and the outward eye, his art makes us highly conscious of how total a response is called for on our part. Bottom, describing what he calls his "dream" of transformation in *A Midsummer Night's Dream*, tells us that:

> "The eye of man hath not heard, the ear of man
> hath not seen, man's hand is not able to taste,
> his tongue to conceive, nor his heart to report
> what my dream was."
>
> Act 4 Scene 1

Bottom has had "a most rare vision," that calls out for multimedia and beyond. We need an eye that can hear, an ear that can see, a hand able to taste, a tongue that can think, and a heart that can speak if we are to apprehend Shakespeare. Chorus, speaking the prologue to *King Henry V*, urges us, as audience, to aid the actors, "Piece out our imperfections with your thoughts." And so we must, so extraordinary and vivid are Shakespeare's imaginings.

Macbeth goes into trance-like states, in which he has second sight, "and nothing is/But what is not." We need to hear him, but also to read him, and then we need to see, through his eyes, what cannot be clutched, an imaginary dagger that becomes bloodied, even as he (and we) gaze upon it.

Shakespeare provides an education of all the senses, as well as of the mind and the heart. When, in Act 5 of *Twelfth Night*, Sebastian and the disguised Viola are revealed as identical twins, except for gender, the Duke Orsino cries out:

> "One face, one voice, one habit, and two persons,
> A natural perspective, that is and is not!"
> Act 5 Scene 1

Orsino means that he sees an optical illusion engendered by nature, rather than one produced by a perspective glass, an Elizabethan multimedia toy. Dr. Samuel Johnson, greatest of English critics, commented upon "a natural perspective" that nature so puts on "a show, where shadows seem realities, where that which 'is not' appears like that which 'is.'" I think that Johnson shrewdly realizes that *Twelfth Night* is a compound toy, a distorting mirror whirling in circles, like a top. This confirms the clown Feste's remark in the play, when he says of Malvolio's predicament, "and thus the whirligig of time brings on his revenges." Shakespeare again anticipates the puzzles, games, and discoveries that children and adults bring to him, and find in him ever more richly than they could have expected.

Mercutio, the bawdy wit of *Romeo and Juliet*, sums up the multimedia prophecy of Shakespeare in his wonderful speech about Queen Mab (Act 1 Scene 4). When Mercutio says of this mischievous fairy that, "Her chariot is an empty hazelnut, made by the joiner squirrel," Shakespeare intends to startle us into a new way of seeing. That may be why Shakespeare is most essential to all of us. He showed us first that all our supposed facts are really interfaces.

Harold Bloom

HISTORICAL BACKGROUND

by Jane Buckland,
Educational Consultant

William Shakespeare's career as an actor and playwright began when he moved to London from Stratford-upon-Avon around 1590. While his family stayed in Stratford, Shakespeare became a wealthy and popular writer and part owner of London's Globe Theatre.

Permanent theaters were new at the time, and Shakespeare's plays were among the first to be performed in them. At the time, acting companies were made up entirely of male actors, with boys playing the female roles.

Shakespeare's plays were popular with ordinary people who came to see his performances at The Globe, The Curtain, and The Theatre. They were also performed for England's aristocracy, and Shakespeare was a favorite of both Queen Elizabeth I and King James I of England. James I liked Shakespeare's acting company so much that he allowed them the honor of calling themselves The King's Men.

Romeo and Juliet was written sometime around 1595, early in Shakespeare's career as a playwright. It was perhaps only his second tragedy, but nonetheless has come to be regarded as among his best. It is certainly one of his most famous plays, and its continuing popularity has ensured regular performances throughout its 400-year history.

One notable aspect of the play, and perhaps one of the reasons for its popularity and success, is that it was one of the first tragedies to deal with the subject of love. Most tragedies of the time used the downfall of kings or emperors as their theme. Love was the subject matter of comedies.

This may explain why the story of Romeo and Juliet can seem almost modern. Its origins, however, date back even earlier than Shakespeare. Versions of this story adapted from an old folktale had been around for at least a hundred years before Shakespeare was writing.

Shakespeare's main source was Arthur Brooke's 1562 poem entitled *The Tragical History of Romeus and Juliet*, a poem which itself was a translation of a French story, which was in turn taken from various Italian tales. Shakespeare made many substantial changes to Brooke's poem, however, and certainly deserves credit for authorship of the play. Most significantly, Shakespeare made his Juliet only 13, not 16 as in Brooke's poem, and developed the characters of Nurse and Mercutio and, to a lesser extent, Paris.

It was not unusual in Shakespeare's time for girls to marry young. It would have been shocking, however, for a girl as young as Juliet to choose her own husband. Her father would have chosen him for her and she would have been expected to obey and be grateful. This happens in the play when Lord Capulet decides Juliet should marry Paris, and explains his anger with his daughter when she refuses to do as he says (Act 3 Scene 5).

Shakespeare sets his play in Italy at a time when each of the towns, such as Verona and Mantua, were ruled by their own princes like small, individual countries. The inhabitants of these city-states felt themselves to be as separate as the citizens of, say, France and Turkey today. When Romeo is banished to another city, it is a terrible punishment and, of course, there are no quick means of communication such as telephones or even a postal service. Any messages have to be carried by hand by someone traveling between the cities and the failure to send a letter toward the end of the play has fatal consequences.

In the hot square of Verona during the play, there is a great deal of tension and violence. The two families, the Capulets and the Montagues, have been feuding for years and although everyone seems to have forgotten the original reason, the fighting goes on. Modern versions of *Romeo and Juliet* have been set in Northern Ireland, among New York gangs (as in the musical *West Side Story*), or wherever two groups of people live closely together but believe themselves to be very different.

In the final scene, it is only the tragic deaths of these young people, the children of the two families, that bring everyone to their senses and stop the feud. In the end, we feel that here there is "much to do with hate but more with love." The passionate story of the two young lovers who meet in secret and who, in the end, choose to die rather than live without each other is one that moves people as much today as we can suppose it did in Elizabethan times.

THE STORY OF
ROMEO & JULIET
A tale of tragic love

INTRODUCTION

Shakespeare's language is four centuries old. Many of the words he used have changed in meaning or disappeared from common use and some phrases can be difficult to understand for modern readers. It can be helpful to know the basic story line of the play before you read the original text or even before you see a theater or film production.

The aim of this story is just that—to help you understand what you are reading when you approach the play text. In this version of the story the action closely follows the play. Act and scene references are included so that you can look things up in the play text while reading the story and vice versa. However, some artistic license has been taken, in much the same way that actors and directors bring their own ideas to a performance of a Shakespearean play. Not every scene from the play is included as some of them are not essential to understanding the plot.

Any quotations in the story are taken directly from the play. Many of these are the more famous lines and are explained in the text if their meaning is not obvious.

Reading the story will help you to play the games on the CD-ROM, but if you want to know all the answers you will need to look at the play itself. Have fun. Entertainment is what Shakespeare is all about!

THE STORY

Act 1 Scene 1

One sweltering July afternoon, two servants of the rich Capulet family were walking through Verona's narrow streets. As they discussed the long-standing feud between the Capulets and their bitter enemies, the Montague family, they saw two servants of the Montagues coming towards them. Hostile looks were exchanged, then insults and, as other members of the two families turned up, a violent brawl broke out.

It wasn't long before the noise had woken half the people in the city from their siestas and Prince Escalus and the local police were in the square breaking up the fight. The Prince was furious with the perpetrators and decreed that if any Capulets or Montagues were caught fighting in the streets again, they would be executed.

Act 1 Scene 2 It was a tradition in the Capulet family to have a great feast at this time of year, and a servant was sent around Verona with a list of guests to invite. However, being unable to read, the servant stopped a couple of young men to ask whose names were on the list. The pair that he approached were Benvolio and his friend Romeo, both of the Montague family.

Romeo took the list and read it. Among the guests was a girl named Rosaline. Romeo thought Rosaline the most beautiful girl he'd ever seen and was hopelessly in love with her, but so far, Rosaline had not returned his affection. Benvolio didn't think Rosaline was worth half the heartache Romeo had spent on her, and frequently teased him about it.

Not knowing they were Montagues, the servant invited Romeo and Benvolio to the party as a way to thank them for their help. Here was a chance for Romeo to meet Rosaline again and he jumped at it. Benvolio said he would go with Romeo to the party and show him that there were many girls far more beautiful than Rosaline.

"Compare her face with some that I shall show, and I will make thee think thy swan a crow," said Benvolio.

As it wouldn't be safe for Montagues to be seen at a Capulet party, the two young men decided to wear masks to disguise themselves.

Act 1 Scene 3 In the Capulet house, last minute preparations for the party were being made. Dressed and ready for the evening, Lady Capulet called her daughter Juliet to her room. At thirteen years old, Juliet was just reaching marriageable age, and because she was the sole heir to the vast Capulet fortune, her parents took great interest in her suitors.

Lady Capulet told her daughter that a young man named Paris had recently asked about the possibility of marriage to Juliet. Her father had been very impressed by him and had invited him to the feast so that he and Juliet might meet. Lady Capulet added that Juliet should consider Paris as a potential husband. Rather reluctantly, Juliet agreed.

Act 1 Scene 4 Outside the Capulet house, Romeo, Benvolio, and another friend, Mercutio, chatted together before they joined the party. Romeo mentioned a disturbing premonition he'd had that the party would be the beginning of a fatal chain of events. Laughing at his emotional friend, Mercutio persuaded Romeo not to worry, and they put on their masks and entered the home of their rivals.

Act 1 Scene 5
Leaving his companions, Romeo pushed through the throng of guests in search of Rosaline, but couldn't find her. Instead, as he scanned the female faces around him, his eyes fell upon another girl, so beautiful that he stopped in his tracks and stared. It was Juliet.

"O, she doth teach the torches to burn bright!" he said to himself, searching for words that would describe such radiance. "It seems she hangs upon the cheek of night as a rich jewel in an Ethiop's ear; beauty too rich for use, for earth too dear!"

In his reverie, Romeo spoke aloud, and Tybalt, a blood thirsty young Capulet who stood nearby, recognized his voice. Planning to cut down the impertinent gate-crasher, Tybalt sent a servant for his sword. But before the boy had returned, Lord Capulet noticed something was annoying his cousin.

"'Tis he, that villain Romeo," said Tybalt.

Capulet would not allow violence to ruin the party and forbade Tybalt to go near Romeo. His blood boiling with fury, Tybalt vowed to himself that he would teach Romeo a lesson for this insult to the Capulet household.

Meanwhile, Romeo had approached Juliet. He took her by the hand and guided her into the shadows behind a pillar.

"If I profane with my unworthiest hand this holy shrine," he said, "the gentle sin is this: my lips, two blushing pilgrims, ready stand to smooth that rough touch with a tender kiss."

He raised his mask and Juliet was as enchanted by Romeo as he was by her. They kissed. Then, abruptly, they were interrupted by Juliet's nurse with a message that her mother was looking for her.

Juliet ran off to speak with her mother and Romeo asked Nurse who it was that he'd just held in his arms. The young man was shocked to discover that he'd fallen for a Capulet. Later, Nurse told Juliet that Romeo was a Montague, and she, too, was devastated.

"My only love sprung from my only hate!" she said sadly to herself; "Too early seen unknown, and known too late."

Act 2 Scene 1
The party came to an end and the guests started to leave. Romeo was so besotted with his new love that he felt he had to see her again. He slipped away from the departing guests and climbed over the wall into the Capulets' orchard.

Act 2 Scene 2 Romeo approached the house and hid behind a large tree, gazing longingly at the open windows. A moment later a curtain fluttered and Juliet appeared on a balcony.

"O Romeo, Romeo! Wherefore art thou Romeo?" she cried into the night; "Deny thy father and refuse thy name! Or, if thou wilt not, be but sworn my love, and I'll no longer be a Capulet."

Romeo moved toward the house until he was standing directly beneath the balcony.

"What's in a name?" continued Juliet. "That which we call a rose by any other name would smell as sweet."

Romeo could keep silent no longer, and in the darkness the two young people exchanged promises of their eternal and undying love. Caught in a whirlwind of passion, they decided to marry as soon as they could. Then, reluctantly, they parted.

"Good night, good night!" whispered Juliet. "Parting is such sweet sorrow."

Act 2 Scene 3 Romeo went straight to Friar Lawrence to arrange the wedding. The sun was just rising as he arrived and the Friar was already up, gathering herbs from the monastery garden. Although he was surprised by the swift change in Romeo's affections, after all, Romeo had been in love with Rosaline only the day before, the Friar agreed to perform the wedding, believing it might help to end the feud between the Capulets and the Montagues.

Act 2 Scene 4
Act 2 Scene 6 A message was passed to Juliet to be at the monastery that afternoon and the ceremony went ahead as planned.

Act 3 Scene 1 After the wedding, Juliet had to return home. Romeo was also heading home, when he encountered Benvolio and Mercutio arguing with Tybalt in the street. Tybalt, who was looking for Romeo to make good his vow of the night before, pushed him roughly against a wall.

"Romeo," he snarled, "the love I bear thee can afford no better term than this—thou art a villain."

Having just married Juliet, Romeo had no wish to argue with a Capulet and tried to make peace with Tybalt. Mercutio didn't like to hear such submissive words from his friend and, drawing his sword, challenged Tybalt to defend himself.

After a bout of vicious fighting, Tybalt stabbed Mercutio in the side. He then ran away, leaving Benvolio and Romeo to see to the injured man. Mercutio looked at his wound.

"No, 'tis not so deep as a well, nor so wide as a church door; but 'tis enough, 'twill serve," he groaned, and within minutes he was dead.

A moment later, Tybalt returned to the scene and Romeo, furious at the death of his friend, drew his sword and lunged at him. Tybalt had barely pulled his sword from its scabbard when he received a fatal wound and fell to the ground, gurgling a bloody oath as he died. Romeo then made his escape, leaving Benvolio to explain to the police what had happened.

News of the fight spread very quickly and soon a large crowd had gathered. Lady Capulet was there grieving for the loss of Tybalt and demanding Romeo be sentenced to death. However, Benvolio persuaded the Prince that Tybalt had started the fight, and Romeo was declared banished from Verona.

Act 3 Scene 2

In the Capulet house, Nurse broke the bad news to Juliet.

"O serpent heart, hid with a flowering face!" cried Juliet in anguish. "Did ever dragon keep so fair a cave?"

Even though she was horrified that Romeo had killed her cousin, she still could not help but adore him. What could she do? Nurse offered to go and find Romeo, knowing that he was in hiding at the monastery.

Act 3 Scene 3

In Friar Lawrence's cell, Romeo declared that he would rather be dead than live without Juliet.

"O deadly sin! O rude unthankfulness!" cried the Friar, shocked that Romeo could say such a thing. His efforts to comfort the distraught young man fell on deaf ears, and Romeo hurled himself to the floor, beating his fists on the cold stone.

Nurse arrived and Romeo returned to his senses a little, but when he heard about Juliet's grief and sadness, he drew his dagger in an attempt to stab himself. Before he could use it, however, Nurse snatched it away and held it out of his reach. Friar Lawrence was outraged by Romeo's selfishness.

"Wilt thou slay thyself? And slay thy lady that in thy life lives, by doing damnèd hate upon thyself?" he said, and told Romeo that he should count himself an extremely lucky man.

Having at last calmed him down, Friar Lawrence decided what Romeo must do. He should spend the night with Juliet as planned, but must leave her before the morning and escape to Mantua. He was to spend his exile there, until the Friar had sorted things out in Verona. To the Friar's relief, Romeo at last saw sense in this plan.

Act 3 Scene 5

It was still dark when Romeo, awakened by birdsong, rose from Juliet's bed and began to get dressed.

"Wilt thou be gone?" asked Juliet, her voice soft and slurred with sleep. "It is not yet near day. It was the nightingale, and not the lark, that pierced the fearful hollow of thine ear."

"It was the lark," said Romeo, "the herald of the morn."
He dared stay no longer.

"Farewell, farewell!" he said, climbing over the balcony wall.
"One kiss, and I'll descend."

Juliet was still standing on the balcony when her mother came in, saying she had some good news. Her father had decided that she would be married to Paris on Thursday. Juliet was horrified and refused to agree to the wedding. She wouldn't change her mind even when old Capulet came to see what all the fuss was about. Juliet's impudence made him very angry as he was not used to such behavior. He roared at his daughter, "Hang thee, young baggage! Disobedient wretch! I tell thee what: get thee to church o' Thursday, or never after look me in the face!"

Juliet burst into tears and her father stormed out of the room, followed by Lady Capulet. Nurse tried hard to persuade Juliet to forget about Romeo and do as her father wished, but she would not listen. Juliet decided to ask Friar Lawrence for advice and immediately set off for the monastery.

Act 4 Scene 1   Friar Lawrence was almost as concerned as Juliet to hear about the planned wedding because he would be expected to perform the ceremony. This he could not do, as it was illegal to solemnize, or perform, a bigamous marriage. How could the problem be resolved? It was hardly a good time to announce Juliet's marriage to Romeo.

As he considered all this, Juliet produced a dagger and threatened to kill herself rather than marry Paris.

"Hold, daughter," said the Friar, "I do spy a kind of hope." He explained that he would give Juliet a potion which would send her into a coma for forty-two hours. If she took this the night before the wedding, she would appear to be dead the following day and her body would be taken to the Capulet vault. Friar Lawrence would inform Romeo of the plan, who would return to Verona to take Juliet from the vault just as she was regaining consciousness. Together they would escape to Mantua.

Juliet jumped at the idea, and Friar Lawrence gave her the potion, saying he would immediately send a messenger to Mantua with a letter for Romeo.

Act 4 Scene 2   When she returned home, Juliet met her father and, as the Friar had instructed, told him that she'd changed her mind and now agreed to marry Paris. Lord Capulet was overjoyed and decided that the wedding should happen sooner. It was now to take place the next day!

Act 4 Scene 3	In her bedroom, Juliet sat staring at the flask of potion in her hands, uneasy thoughts running through her mind. What if the Friar was trying to poison her to avoid performing an illegal marriage? What if the potion didn't work at all?
	But then, what else could she do but try it? Before her nerve failed her, she opened the little bottle and swallowed its contents down.
Act 4 Scene 5	Early the next morning, Nurse came to wake Juliet.
	"Alas, alas! Help, help! My lady's dead!" she cried, discovering the young girl's cold and lifeless body.
	Her cries quickly alerted the household and Juliet's parents raced into the room.
	"Alack the day, she's dead, she's dead, she's dead!" howled Lady Capulet.
Act 5 Scene 1	The shocking news spread across Verona like wildfire and had reached the Montague house within minutes. Immediately, a servant named Balthasar set out to tell Romeo. He arrived in Mantua early the next morning, and found Romeo desperate for information, having not received any news from Friar Lawrence.
	"Is it even so?" asked Romeo, unable to take in the gravity of Balthasar's news. The servant nodded. "Then I defy you, stars!" Romeo cried.
	Intent on ending his life, he found an apothecary, or pharmacist, who would sell him poison and set off for Verona to join Juliet in her tomb.
Act 5 Scene 2	The poor monk whom Friar Lawrence had entrusted with the letter for Romeo had been unable to leave Verona. The previous day, he had visited a house where suspected victims of the plague lived, and had been locked up in quarantine for the past twenty-four hours. The letter he carried had never reached Romeo.
	"Unhappy fortune!" cried Friar Lawrence when he heard. Grabbing a crowbar and shovel, he set out for the Capulet vault to open it before Juliet awoke.
Act 5 Scene 3	Night had fallen over Verona's cemetery. Sick at heart with grief, Paris was at the Capulets' tomb mourning his dead bride-to-be when a noise disturbed him. He retreated into the shadows, not wanting to meet anyone in his sorrow. Two men approached the vault and, by the light of their lantern, Paris saw it was Romeo and Balthasar. Sending Balthasar away, Romeo took up a crowbar and began wrenching open the tomb. Paris couldn't stand to see this wanton act of vandalism.

Wasn't it Romeo who had killed Tybalt and, indirectly, Juliet, who had died of grief for her dead cousin? Now what horrors did the foul murderer wish to commit on their corpses?

Rising out of the shadows, Paris cried, "Stop thy unhallowed toil, vile Montague!"

The desperate Romeo would let nothing come between him and his wish to lie with Juliet, and pleaded with Paris to let him be. Paris would not leave him, and the two men drew their daggers and fought. Soon Paris was lying dead on the ground.

At last, Romeo entered the tomb and, after dragging Paris' body in with him, knelt down beside Juliet. Speaking softly to his love in the vault's dank gloom, Romeo drank his poison. As the drug began to work, he kissed Juliet and said his last words, "Thus with a kiss I die."

When Friar Lawrence entered the tomb a few minutes later, Romeo and Paris both lay dead on the floor and Juliet was just waking.

"O comfortable Friar!" said Juliet as she gradually came to. "Where is my lord?"

Horrified at how his plan had gone so terribly wrong, the Friar tried to usher Juliet out of the tomb, but she had already seen Romeo's body on the floor and would not leave him. At that moment, voices were heard outside and the wretched Friar, frightened out of his wits, ran off, leaving Juliet on her own.

Juliet saw the bottle of poison still clasped in Romeo's hand and looked to see if there might be enough left for her. Finding the bottle empty, she took his dagger and plunged it into her heart.

The voices that Friar Lawrence had heard belonged to the night watchmen. They soon discovered the bodies in the tomb and caught the Friar with his crowbar and shovel. Prince Escalus was called and he, along with the Capulets, Lord Montague, and a large crowd of onlookers, went to the vault.

Friar Lawrence was called upon, and he and Balthasar, who had witnessed the night's events, explained what had happened. With the Prince's mediation, old Capulet and Montague made up their differences and promised that each would have a statue of the other's child built in the town.

The feud between the Montagues and the Capulets was finally over, but at what cost. "For never was a story of more woe," said the Prince, "than this of Juliet and her Romeo."

CHARACTERS IN THE PLAY

The house of Capulet

LORD CAPULET	Head of the Capulet family
LADY CAPULET	Lord Capulet's wife
JULIET	The Capulets' daughter
TYBALT	Juliet's cousin
NURSE	The woman who looks after Juliet
COUSIN CAPULET	An old relative of Lord Capulet
PETER	Nurse's servant
SAMPSON	A servant
GREGORY	A servant

The house of Montague

LORD MONTAGUE	Head of the Montague family
LADY MONTAGUE	Lord Montague's wife
ROMEO	The Montagues' son
BENVOLIO	Romeo's cousin and friend
BALTHASAR	Romeo's servant
ABRAHAM	A servant

The Prince's household

PRINCE ESCALUS   Prince of Verona

MERCUTIO   A relative of the Prince, Romeo's friend

PARIS   A relative of the Prince and a local Count

MERCUTIO'S PAGE   who helps Mercutio when he is dying

PARIS' PAGE   who witnesses events at the Capulet vault

FRIAR LAWRENCE   A Franciscan Friar who helps Romeo and Juliet

FRIAR JOHN   A Franciscan Friar

APOTHECARY   who sells Romeo poison in Mantua

THREE WATCHMEN   who discover the scene in the Capulet vault

THREE MUSICIANS   who are supposed to play at Juliet's wedding to Paris

THE CHORUS   which summarizes events in the play

Citizens
Party Guests
Pages
Servants
Attendants

ACT 1

PROLOGUE

Enter CHORUS

PROLOGUE
THE CHORUS TELLS US ABOUT THE LONG-STANDING FEUD BETWEEN THE MONTAGUE AND CAPULET FAMILIES. WE ARE GIVEN AN OUTLINE OF THE STORY, AND WARNED THAT TWO YOUNG LOVERS WILL DIE BEFORE THE FEUD ENDS.

DISK LINK
Before you read farther, why not find out who's who in MEET THE CHARACTERS?

CHORUS
　　Two households, both alike in dignity,
　　　　In fair Verona, where we lay our scene,
　　From ancient grudge break to new mutiny,
　　　　Where civil blood makes civil hands unclean.
　　From forth the fatal loins of these two foes
　　　　A pair of star-crossed lovers take their life;
　　Whose misadventured piteous overthrows
　　　　Doth with their death bury their parents' strife.
　　The fearful passage of their death-marked love,
　　　　And the continuance of their parents' rage,
　　Which, but their children's end, nought could remove,
　　　　Is now the two hours' traffic of our stage;
　　The which if you with patient ears attend,
　　　　What here shall miss, our toil shall strive to mend.

Exit

SCENE 1

A street in Verona

ACT 1 SCENE 1
A FIGHT BETWEEN THE MONTAGUES AND THE CAPULETS BREAKS OUT. THE PRINCE INTERVENES AND THREATENS DEATH FOR ANYONE CAUGHT FIGHTING AGAIN. MONTAGUE AND HIS WIFE ARE ANXIOUS ABOUT THEIR SON, ROMEO. THEY ASK BENVOLIO ABOUT HIM, AND HE AGREES THAT ROMEO HAS BEEN ACTING STRANGELY. BENVOLIO SAYS HE WILL FIND OUT ALL HE CAN. ROMEO ENTERS AND TELLS BENVOLIO THAT HE IS IN LOVE WITH A GIRL CALLED ROSALINE WHO DOES NOT LOVE HIM.

Enter SAMPSON *and* GREGORY, *Servants of the house of Capulet, armed with swords and shields*

SAMPSON
　　Gregory, on my word, we'll not carry coals.
GREGORY
　　No, for then we should be colliers.
SAMPSON
　　I mean, and we be in choler, we'll draw.
GREGORY
　　Ay, while you live, draw your neck out of the collar.
SAMPSON
　　I strike quickly, being moved.
GREGORY
　　But thou art not quickly moved to strike.
SAMPSON
　　A dog of the house of Montague moves me.

GREGORY

To move is to stir; and to be valiant is to stand.
Therefore, if thou art moved, thou runn'st away.

SAMPSON

A dog of that house shall move me to stand. I will take
the wall of any man or maid of Montague's.

GREGORY

That shows thee a weak slave; for the weakest goes
to the wall.

SAMPSON

'Tis true; and therefore women, being the weaker vessels,
are ever thrust to the wall. Therefore I will push Montague's
men from the wall and thrust his maids to the wall.

GREGORY

The quarrel is between our masters and us their men.

SAMPSON

'Tis all one. I will show myself a tyrant. When I have fought
with the men, I will be civil with the maids—I will cut off
their heads.

GREGORY

The heads of the maids?

SAMPSON

Ay, the heads of the maids, or their maidenheads; take it
in what sense thou wilt.

GREGORY

They must take it in sense that feel it.

SAMPSON

Me they shall feel while I am able to stand; and 'tis known
I am a pretty piece of flesh.

GREGORY

'Tis well thou art not fish; if thou hadst, thou hadst been
poor John. Draw thy tool! here comes two of the house of
the Montagues.

Enter ABRAHAM *and Balthasar, Servants of the house of Montague*

SAMPSON

My naked weapon is out. Quarrel, I will back thee.

GREGORY

How? Turn thy back and run?

SAMPSON

Fear me not.

GREGORY

No, marry. I fear thee!

SAMPSON

Let us take the law of our sides; let them begin.

GREGORY

I will frown as I pass by, and let them take it as they list.

SAMPSON

Nay, as they dare. I will bite my thumb at them, which is disgrace to them, if they bear it.

ABRAHAM

Do you bite your thumb at us, Sir?

SAMPSON

I do bite my thumb, Sir.

ABRAHAM

Do you bite your thumb at us, Sir?

SAMPSON

(*Aside to* GREGORY) Is the law of our side, if I say "ay?"

GREGORY

(*Aside to* SAMPSON) No.

SAMPSON

(*Replying to* ABRAHAM) No, Sir, I do not bite my thumb at you, Sir, but I bite my thumb, Sir.

GREGORY

Do you quarrel, Sir?

ABRAHAM

Quarrel Sir? No, Sir.

SAMPSON

But if you do, Sir, I am for you. I serve as good a man as you.

ABRAHAM

No better?

SAMPSON

Well, Sir.

Enter BENVOLIO

GREGORY

(*Interrupting* SAMPSON *as he sees* TYBALT *approaching*) Say "better." Here comes one of my master's kinsmen.

SAMPSON

(*To* ABRAHAM) Yes, better, Sir.

ABRAHAM

You lie.

SAMPSON

Draw, if you be men. Gregory, remember thy swashing blow.

DISK LINK
There's a quotation on this page that will help you play WHO SAID WHAT?

They fight, BENVOLIO *tries to separate them*

BENVOLIO
Part, fools!
Put up your swords. You know not what you do.

Beats down their swords. Enter TYBALT

TYBALT
What, art thou drawn among these heartless hinds?
Turn thee, Benvolio, look upon thy death.
BENVOLIO
I do but keep the peace. Put up thy sword,
Or manage it to part these men with me.
TYBALT
What, drawn, and talk of peace? I hate the word
As I hate hell, all Montagues, and thee.
Have at thee, coward!

They fight. Enter several members of both houses, who join the fray; then enter CITIZENS *with clubs*

FIRST CITIZEN
Clubs, bills, and partisans! Strike! Beat them down!
Down with the Capulets! Down with the Montagues!

Enter CAPULET *in his nightgown, and* LADY CAPULET

CAPULET
What noise is this? Give me my long sword, ho!
LADY CAPULET
A crutch, a crutch! Why call you for a sword?
CAPULET
My sword, I say! Old Montague is come,
And flourishes his blade in spite of me.

Enter MONTAGUE *and* LADY MONTAGUE

MONTAGUE
Thou villain Capulet. (*To* LADY MONTAGUE) Hold me not, let me go.
LADY MONTAGUE
Thou shalt not stir one foot to seek a foe.

Enter PRINCE ESCALUS, *with Attendants*

PRINCE
Rebellious subjects, enemies to peace,
Profaners of this neighbour-stainèd steel—
Will they not hear? What, ho! you men, you beasts,
That quench the fire of your pernicious rage
With purple fountains issuing from your veins,
On pain of torture, from those bloody hands
Throw your mistempered weapons to the ground,
And hear the sentence of your movèd Prince.
Three civil brawls, bred of an airy word,
By thee, old Capulet, and Montague,
Have thrice disturbed the quiet of our streets,
And made Verona's ancient citizens
Cast by their grave beseeming ornaments,
To wield old partisans, in hands as old,
Cankered with peace, to part your cankered hate.
If ever you disturb our streets again,
Your lives shall pay the forfeit of the peace.
For this time, all the rest depart away.
You, Capulet, shall go along with me;
And, Montague, come you this afternoon,
To know our further pleasure in this case,
To old Freetown, our common judgement place.
Once more, on pain of death, all men depart.

Exeunt all but MONTAGUE, LADY MONTAGUE, *and* BENVOLIO

MONTAGUE
Who set this ancient quarrel new abroach?
Speak, nephew, were you by when it began?
BENVOLIO
Here were the servants of your adversary,
And yours, close fighting ere I did approach.
I drew to part them. In the instant came
The fiery Tybalt, with his sword prepared,
Which, as he breathed defiance to my ears,
He swung about his head and cut the winds,
Who nothing hurt withal hissed him in scorn.
While we were interchanging thrusts and blows,
Came more and more and fought on part and part,
Till the Prince came, who parted either part.
LADY MONTAGUE
O, where is Romeo? Saw you him today?

Right glad I am he was not at this fray.

BENVOLIO

Madam, an hour before the worshipped sun
Peered forth the golden window of the east,
A troubled mind drove me to walk abroad;
Where, underneath the grove of sycamore
That westward rooteth from this city side,
So early walking did I see your son.
Towards him I made, but he was ware of me
And stole into the covert of the wood.
I, measuring his affections by my own,
That most are busied when they're most alone,
Pursued my humour not pursuing his,
And gladly shunned who gladly fled from me.

MONTAGUE

Many a morning hath he there been seen,
With tears augmenting the fresh morning's dew,
Adding to clouds more clouds with his deep sighs;
But all so soon as the all-cheering sun
Should in the farthest east begin to draw
The shady curtains from Aurora's bed,
Away from light steals home my heavy son,
And private in his chamber pens himself,
Shuts up his windows, locks fair daylight out
And makes himself an artificial night.
Black and portentous must this humour prove,
Unless good counsel may the cause remove.

BENVOLIO

My noble uncle, do you know the cause?

MONTAGUE

I neither know it nor can learn of him.

BENVOLIO

Have you importuned him by any means?

MONTAGUE

Both by myself and many other friends;
But he, his own affections' counsellor,
Is to himself—I will not say how true—
But to himself so secret and so close,
So far from sounding and discovery,
As is the bud bit with an envious worm,
Ere he can spread his sweet leaves to the air,
Or dedicate his beauty to the sun.
Could we but learn from whence his sorrows grow,
We would as willingly give cure as know.

Enter ROMEO

BENVOLIO
See, where he comes. So please you, step aside;
I'll know his grievance, or be much denied.

MONTAGUE
I would thou wert so happy by thy stay,
To hear true shrift. Come, madam, let's away.

Exeunt MONTAGUE *and* LADY MONTAGUE

BENVOLIO
Good morrow, cousin.

ROMEO
                                        Is the day so young?

BENVOLIO
But new struck nine.

ROMEO
                                  Ay me! Sad hours seem long.
Was that my father that went hence so fast?

BENVOLIO
It was. What sadness lengthens Romeo's hours?

ROMEO
Not having that which, having, makes them short.

BENVOLIO
In love?

ROMEO
Out—

BENVOLIO
Of love?

ROMEO
Out of her favour, where I am in love.

BENVOLIO
Alas, that love, so gentle in his view,
Should be so tyrannous and rough in proof!

ROMEO
Alas, that love, whose view is muffled still,
Should, without eyes, see pathways to his will!
Where shall we dine? O me! What fray was here?
Yet tell me not, for I have heard it all.
Here's much to do with hate, but more with love.
Why, then, O brawling love! O loving hate!
O anything of nothing first create.
O heavy lightness! serious vanity!
Misshapen chaos of well-seeming forms.

Feather of lead, bright smoke, cold fire, sick health.
Still-waking sleep, that is not what it is!
This love feel I, that feel no love in this.
Dost thou not laugh?

BENVOLIO

No, coz, I rather weep.

ROMEO

Good heart, at what?

BENVOLIO

At thy good heart's oppression.

ROMEO

Why, such is love's transgression.
Griefs of mine own lie heavy in my breast,
Which thou wilt propagate, to have it pressed
With more of thine. This love that thou hast shown
Doth add more grief to too much of mine own.
Love is a smoke made with the fume of sighs;
Being purged, a fire sparkling in lovers' eyes;
Being vexed, a sea nourished with lovers' tears.
What is it else? a madness most discreet,
A choking gall and a preserving sweet.
Farewell, my coz.

BENVOLIO

Soft! I will go along.
And if you leave me so, you do me wrong.

ROMEO

Tut, I have lost myself; I am not here;
This is not Romeo, he's some other where.

BENVOLIO

Tell me in sadness, who is that you love?

ROMEO

What, shall I groan and tell thee?

BENVOLIO

Groan! why, no.
But sadly tell me who.

ROMEO

Bid a sick man in sadness make his will.
Ah, word ill urged to one that is so ill!
In sadness, cousin, I do love a woman.

BENVOLIO

I aimed so near when I supposed you loved.

ROMEO

A right good mark-man! And she's fair I love.

BENVOLIO

A right fair mark, fair coz, is soonest hit.

ROMEO

Well, in that hit you miss. She'll not be hit
With Cupid's arrow. She hath Dian's wit,
And, in strong proof of chastity well armed,
From love's weak childish bow she lives uncharmed.
She will not stay the siege of loving terms,
Nor bide th' encounter of assailing eyes,
Nor ope her lap to saint-seducing gold.
O, she is rich in beauty, only poor,
That when she dies, with beauty dies her store.

BENVOLIO

Then she hath sworn that she will still live chaste?

ROMEO

She hath, and in that sparing makes huge waste,
For beauty starved with her severity
Cuts beauty off from all posterity.
She is too fair, too wise, wisely too fair,
To merit bliss by making me despair.
She hath forsworn to love, and in that vow
Do I live dead that live to tell it now.

BENVOLIO

Be ruled by me, forget to think of her.

ROMEO

O, teach me how I should forget to think!

BENVOLIO

By giving liberty unto thine eyes.
Examine other beauties.

ROMEO

'Tis the way
To call hers, exquisite, in question more.
These happy masks that kiss fair ladies' brows,
Being black, puts us in mind they hide the fair.
He that is strucken blind cannot forget
The precious treasure of his eyesight lost.
Show me a mistress that is passing fair,
What doth her beauty serve, but as a note
Where I may read who passed that passing fair?
Farewell. Thou canst not teach me to forget.

BENVOLIO

I'll pay that doctrine, or else die in debt.

Exeunt

ACT 1 SCENE 2

COUNT PARIS ASKS CAPULET FOR HIS DAUGHTER JULIET'S HAND IN MARRIAGE. CAPULET IS UNSURE BECAUSE SHE IS VERY YOUNG, BUT INVITES PARIS TO A PARTY HE IS GIVING THAT NIGHT. IF PARIS CAN WIN JULIET'S LOVE, HER FATHER WILL AGREE TO THE MATCH. ROMEO AND BENVOLIO FIND OUT ABOUT THE PARTY AND DECIDE TO GO ALONG. ROSALINE WILL BE THERE, BUT SO WILL MANY OTHER BEAUTIFUL WOMEN, AND BENVOLIO THINKS THAT ROMEO MAY FIND ONE OF THEM MORE ATTRACTIVE THAN ROSALINE.

SCENE 2

The same street in Verona

Enter CAPULET, PARIS, *and a* SERVANT

CAPULET
But Montague is bound as well as I,
In penalty alike; and 'tis not hard, I think,
For men so old as we to keep the peace.

PARIS
Of honourable reckoning are you both,
And pity 'tis you lived at odds so long.
But now, my lord, what say you to my suit?

CAPULET
But saying o'er what I have said before:
My child is yet a stranger in the world,
She hath not seen the change of fourteen years,
Let two more summers wither in their pride,
Ere we may think her ripe to be a bride.

PARIS
Younger than she are happy mothers made.

CAPULET
And too soon marred are those so early made.
Earth hath swallowèd all my hopes but she;
She is the hopeful lady of my earth.
But woo her, gentle Paris, get her heart,
My will to her consent is but a part.
And she agreed, within her scope of choice
Lies my consent and fair according voice.
This night I hold an old accustomed feast,
Whereto I have invited many a guest,
Such as I love; and you, among the store,
One more, most welcome, makes my number more.
At my poor house look to behold this night
Earth-treading stars that make dark heaven light.
Such comfort as do lusty young men feel
When well-apparelled April on the heel
Of limping winter treads, even such delight
Among fresh female buds shall you this night
Inherit at my house. Hear all, all see,
And like her most whose merit most shall be;
Which, on more view of many, mine being one,
May stand in number, though in reckoning none,

Come, go with me. (*To the* SERVANT, *giving him a paper*) Go,
    sirrah, trudge about
Through fair Verona; find those persons out
Whose names are written there, and to them say,
My house and welcome on their pleasure stay.

Exeunt CAPULET *and* PARIS

SERVANT
Find them out whose names are written here! It is written,
that the shoemaker should meddle with his yard, and the
tailor with his last, the fisher with his pencil, and the painter
with his nets; but I am sent to find those persons whose
names are here writ, and can never find what names the
writing person hath here writ. I must to the learned. (*He sees*
BENVOLIO *and* ROMEO *approaching*) In good time.

Enter BENVOLIO *and* ROMEO

BENVOLIO
Tut, man, one fire burns out another's burning,
One pain is lessened by another's anguish;
Turn giddy, and be holp by backward turning;
One desperate grief cures with another's languish.
Take thou some new infection to thy eye,
And the rank poison of the old will die.

ROMEO
Your plantain leaf is excellent for that.

BENVOLIO
For what, I pray thee?

ROMEO
                For your broken shin.

BENVOLIO
Why, Romeo, art thou mad?

ROMEO
Not mad, but bound more than a madman is;
Shut up in prison, kept without my food,
Whipped and tormented and—Good e'en, good fellow.

SERVANT
God gi' good e'en. I pray, Sir, can you read?

ROMEO
Ay, mine own fortune in my misery.

SERVANT
Perhaps you have learned it without book. But, I
pray, can you read anything you see?

ROMEO

Ay, if I know the letters and the language.

SERVANT

Ye say honestly. Rest you merry! (*He moves off*)

ROMEO

Stay, fellow; I can read. (*Reads the list*)
"Signor Martino and his wife and daughters; County Anselme and his beauteous sisters; the lady widow of Vitruvio; Signor Placentio and his lovely nieces; Mercutio and his brother Valentine; mine uncle Capulet, his wife and daughters; my fair niece Rosaline and Livia; Signor Valentio and his cousin Tybalt; Lucio and the lively Helena."
A fair assembly. Whither should they come?

SERVANT

Up.

ROMEO

Whither? To supper?

SERVANT

To our house.

ROMEO

Whose house?

SERVANT

My master's.

ROMEO

Indeed, I should have asked you that before.

SERVANT

Now I'll tell you without asking. My master is the great rich Capulet; and if you be not of the house of Montagues, I pray, come and crush a cup of wine. Rest you merry!

Exit SERVANT

BENVOLIO

At this same ancient feast of Capulet's
Sups the fair Rosaline whom thou so loves,
With all the admired beauties of Verona.
Go thither, and, with unattainted eye,
Compare her face with some that I shall show,
And I will make thee think thy swan a crow.

ROMEO

When the devout religion of mine eye
Maintains such falsehood, then turn tears to fire;
And these, who often drowned could never die,
Transparent heretics, be burnt for liars!
One fairer than my love? The all-seeing sun

DISK LINK
Guess what Shakespeare's more difficult words and phrases mean in the GLOSSARY GAME.

Ne'er saw her match since first the world begun.

BENVOLIO
Tut, you saw her fair, none else being by,
Herself poised with herself in either eye;
But in that crystal scales let there be weighed
Your lady's love against some other maid
That I will show you shining at this feast,
And she shall scant show well that now shows best.

ROMEO
I'll go along, no such sight to be shown,
But to rejoice in splendour of mine own.

Exeunt

ACT 1 SCENE 3
NURSE TALKS ABOUT JULIET'S
CHILDHOOD. LADY CAPULET TELLS
JULIET THAT SHE HAS A SUITOR, THE
COUNT PARIS, AND URGES HER
DAUGHTER TO TRY TO LIKE HIM.
JULIET DUTIFULLY AGREES.

SCENE 3
A room in Capulet's house

Enter LADY CAPULET *and* NURSE

LADY CAPULET
Nurse, where's my daughter? Call her forth to me.

NURSE
Now, by my maidenhead, at twelve year old,
I bade her come. What, lamb! What, ladybird!
God forbid! Where's this girl? What, Juliet!

Enter JULIET

JULIET
How now? Who calls?

NURSE
Your mother.

JULIET
Madam, I am here. What is your will?

LADY CAPULET
This is the matter: Nurse, give leave awhile,
We must talk in secret. Nurse, come back again;
I have remembered me, thou's hear our counsel.
Thou know'st my daughter's of a pretty age.

NURSE
Faith, I can tell her age unto an hour.

LADY CAPULET
She's not fourteen.

NURSE

I'll lay fourteen of my teeth,
And yet, to my teen be it spoken, I have but four—
She is not fourteen. How long is it now
To Lammastide?

LADY CAPULET

A fortnight and odd days.

NURSE

Even or odd, of all days in the year,
Come Lammas Eve at night shall she be fourteen.
Susan and she (God rest all Christian souls!)
Were of an age. Well, Susan is with God;
She was too good for me. But, as I said,
On Lammas Eve at night shall she be fourteen;
That shall she, marry; I remember it well.
'Tis since the earthquake now eleven years;
And she was weaned (I never shall forget it)
Of all the days of the year, upon that day
For I had then laid wormwood to my dug,
Sitting in the sun under the dovehouse wall.
My lord and you were then at Mantua.
Nay, I do bear a brain. But, as I said,
When it did taste the wormwood on the nipple
Of my dug and felt it bitter, pretty fool,
To see it tetchy and fall out with the dug!
"Shake," quoth the dovehouse! 'Twas no need, I trow,
To bid me trudge.
And since that time it is eleven years,
For then she could stand high lone; nay, by the rood,
She could have run and waddled all about;
For even the day before, she broke her brow,
And then my husband (God be with his soul!
'A was a merry man) took up the child.
"Yea," quoth he, "dost thou fall upon thy face?
Thou wilt fall backward when thou hast more wit,
Wilt thou not, Jule?" And, by my holidame,
The pretty wretch left crying and said "Ay."
To see, now, how a jest shall come about!
I warrant, and I should live a thousand years,
I never should forget it. "Wilt thou not, Jule?" quoth he,
And, pretty fool, it stinted and said "Ay."

LADY CAPULET

Enough of this; I pray thee, hold thy peace.

NURSE
Yes, Madam. Yet I cannot choose but laugh
To think it should leave crying and say "Ay."
And yet, I warrant, it had upon its brow
A bump as big as a young cockerel's stone;
A perilous knock; and it cried bitterly.
"Yea," quoth my husband, "fall'st upon thy face?
Thou wilt fall backward when thou comest to age;
Wilt thou not, Jule?" It stinted and said "Ay."

JULIET
And stint thou too, I pray thee, Nurse, say I.

NURSE
Peace, I have done. God mark thee to his grace!
Thou wast the prettiest babe that e'er I nursed.
And I might live to see thee married once,
I have my wish.

LADY CAPULET
Marry, that "marry" is the very theme
I came to talk of. Tell me, daughter Juliet,
How stands your disposition to be married?

JULIET
It is an honour that I dream not of.

NURSE
An honour! Were not I thine only nurse,
I would say thou hadst sucked wisdom from thy teat.

LADY CAPULET
Well, think of marriage now. Younger than you,
Here in Verona, ladies of esteem,
Are made already mothers. By my count,
I was your mother much upon these years
That you are now a maid. Thus then in brief:
The valiant Paris seeks you for his love.

NURSE
A man, young lady! Lady, such a man
As all the world—why, he's a man of wax.

LADY CAPULET
Verona's summer hath not such a flower.

NURSE
Nay, he's a flower, in faith, a very flower.

LADY CAPULET
What say you? Can you love the gentleman?
This night you shall behold him at our feast.
Read o'er the volume of young Paris' face,
And find delight writ there with beauty's pen;

DISK LINK
Test your knowledge of the play in WALK-THROUGH ROMEO AND JULIET. This quiz will sort the swans from the crows!

Examine every married lineament,
And see how one another lends content;
And what obscured in this fair volume lies,
Find written in the margent of his eyes.
This precious book of love, this unbound lover,
To beautify him, only lacks a cover.
The fish lives in the sea, and 'tis much pride
For fair without, the fair within to hide.
That book in many's eyes doth share the glory,
That in gold clasps locks in the golden story;
So shall you share all that he doth possess,
By having him, making yourself no less.

NURSE
No less? Nay, bigger; women grow by men.

LADY CAPULET
Speak briefly, can you like of Paris' love?

JULIET
I'll look to like, if looking liking move;
But no more deep will I endart mine eye
Than your consent gives strength to make it fly.

Enter SERVANT

SERVANT
Madam, the guests are come, supper served up, you called, my young lady asked for, the Nurse cursed in the pantry, and everything in extremity. I must hence to wait. I beseech you, follow straight.

LADY CAPULET
We follow thee. (*Exit* SERVANT) Juliet, the County stays.

NURSE
Go, girl, seek happy nights to happy days.

Exeunt

ACT 1 SCENE 4
ROMEO, BENVOLIO, AND MERCUTIO
ARE READY TO GO TO THE BALL. THEY
ARE WEARING MASKS SO THAT THEY
WILL NOT BE RECOGNIZED. ROMEO
HAS GRAVE DOUBTS ABOUT GOING,
BUT THE OTHERS TEASE HIM SO MUCH
THAT EVENTUALLY HE AGREES TO GO.

SCENE 4
A street in Verona

Enter ROMEO, MERCUTIO, BENVOLIO, *with five or six Masked men, Torchbearers, and others*

ROMEO
What, shall this speech be spoke for our excuse?
Or shall we on without apology?

BENVOLIO
The date is out of such prolixity.
We'll have no Cupid hoodwinked with a scarf,
Bearing a Tartar's painted bow of lath,
Scaring the ladies like a crowkeeper;
Nor no without-book prologue, faintly spoke
After the prompter, for our entrance;
But let them measure us by what they will,
We'll measure them a measure, and be gone.

ROMEO
Give me a torch. I am not for this ambling.
Being but heavy, I will bear the light.

MERCUTIO
Nay, gentle Romeo, we must have you dance.

ROMEO
Not I, believe me. You have dancing shoes
With nimble soles; I have a soul of lead
So stakes me to the ground I cannot move.

MERCUTIO
You are a lover. Borrow Cupid's wings,
And soar with them above a common bound.

ROMEO
I am too sore empiercèd with his shaft
To soar with his light feathers, and so bound,
I cannot bound a pitch above dull woe.
Under love's heavy burden do I sink.

MERCUTIO
And, to sink in it, should you burden love,
Too great oppression for a tender thing.

ROMEO
Is love a tender thing? It is too rough,
Too rude, too boisterous, and it pricks like thorn.

MERCUTIO
If love be rough with you, be rough with love.

Prick love for pricking, and you beat love down.
Give me a case to put my visage in.
A visor for a visor! What care I
What curious eye doth quote deformities?
Here are the beetle brows shall blush for me.

He puts on a mask

BENVOLIO

Come, knock and enter; and no sooner in,
But every man betake him to his legs.

ROMEO

A torch for me! Let wantons light of heart
Tickle the senseless rushes with their heels,
For I am proverbed with a grandsire phrase,
I'll be a candle-holder, and look on.
The game was ne'er so fair, and I am done.

MERCUTIO

Tut, dun's the mouse, the constable's own word!
If thou art dun, we'll draw thee from the mire
Or, save your reverence, love, wherein thou stick'st
Up to the ears. Come, we burn daylight, ho!

ROMEO

Nay, that's not so.

MERCUTIO

                I mean, Sir, in delay
We waste our lights in vain, like lamps by day.
Take our good meaning, for our judgement sits
Five times in that ere once in our five wits.

ROMEO

And we mean well in going to this masque;
But 'tis no wit to go.

MERCUTIO

                Why, may one ask?

ROMEO

I dreamt a dream tonight.

MERCUTIO

                And so did I.

ROMEO

Well, what was yours?

MERCUTIO

                That dreamers often lie.

ROMEO

In bed asleep, while they do dream things true.

MERCUTIO
O, then, I see Queen Mab hath been with you.

BENVOLIO
Queen Mab? What's she?

MERCUTIO
She is the fairies' midwife, and she comes
In shape no bigger than an agate stone
On the forefinger of an alderman,
Drawn with a team of little atomies
Athwart men's noses as they lie asleep;
Her waggon spokes made of long spiders' legs,
The cover of the wings of grasshoppers,
Her traces of the smallest spider's web;
Her collars of the moonshine's watery beams,
Her whip of cricket's bone, the lash of film,
Her waggoner a small grey-coated gnat,
Not half so big as a round little worm
Pricked from the lazy finger of a maid;
Her chariot is an empty hazelnut
Made by the joiner squirrel or old grub,
Time out o' mind the fairies' coachmakers.
And in this state she gallops night by night
Through lovers' brains, and then they dream of love;
O'er courtiers' knees, that dream on curtsies straight,
O'er lawyers' fingers, who straight dream on fees,
O'er ladies' lips, who straight on kisses dream,
Which oft the angry Mab with blisters plagues,
Because their breaths with sweetmeats tainted are.
Sometime she gallops o'er a courtier's nose,
And then dreams he of smelling out a suit;
And sometime comes she with a tithe-pig's tail
Tickling a parson's nose as 'a lies asleep,
And then dreams he of another benefice.
Sometime she driveth o'er a soldier's neck,
And then dreams he of cutting foreign throats,
Of breaches, ambuscadoes, Spanish blades,
Of healths five-fathom deep; and then anon
Drums in his ear, at which he starts and wakes,
And being thus frighted swears a prayer or two
And sleeps again. This is that very Mab
That plaits the manes of horses in the night,
And bakes the elflocks in foul sluttish hairs,
Which once untangled, much misfortune bodes.
This is the hag, when maids lie on their backs,

That presses them and learns them first to bear,
Making them women of good carriage.
This is she—

ROMEO

               Peace, peace, Mercutio, peace!
Thou talk'st of nothing.

MERCUTIO

                 True, I talk of dreams,
Which are the children of an idle brain,
Begot of nothing but vain fantasy,
Which is as thin of substance as the air
And more inconstant than the wind, who woos
Even now the frozen bosom of the north,
And, being angered, puffs away from thence,
Turning his face to the dew-dropping south.

BENVOLIO

This wind you talk of blows us from ourselves.
Supper is done, and we shall come too late.

ROMEO

I fear, too early; for my mind misgives
Some consequence yet hanging in the stars
Shall bitterly begin his fearful date
With this night's revels, and expire the term
Of a despisèd life closed in my breast
By some vile forfeit of untimely death.
But He, that hath the steerage of my course,
Direct my sail! On, lusty gentlemen.

BENVOLIO

Strike, drum.

Exeunt

SCENE 5
A hall in Capulet's house

Musicians waiting. Enter ROMEO, *and other Masked men, and Torchbearers. Enter two* SERVANTS

FIRST SERVANT

Where's Potpan, that he helps not to take away? He shift a trencher? He scrape a trencher!

DISK LINK
Can you remember all the characters, props, and sound effects in this scene? Test yourself in MAKE A SCENE.

SECOND SERVANT

When good manners shall lie all in one or two men's hands and they unwashed too, 'tis a foul thing.

FIRST SERVANT

Away with the joint-stools, remove the court-cupboard, look to the plate. Good thou, save me a piece of marchpane; and, as thou loves me, let the porter let in Susan Grindstone and Nell.
(*He calls*) Antony, and Potpan!

Enter two Servants, ANTONY *and* POTPAN

ANTONY

Ay, boy, ready.

FIRST SERVANT

You are looked for and called for, asked for and sought for, in the great chamber.

POTPAN

We cannot be here and there too. Cheerly, boys; be brisk awhile, and the longer liver take all.

Exeunt ANTONY *and* POTPAN

Enter CAPULET, LADY CAPULET, JULIET, TYBALT, NURSE, *and others of the house, meeting the Guests and Masked men*

CAPULET

Welcome, gentlemen! Ladies that have their toes
Unplagued with corns will walk a bout with you.
Ah ha, my mistresses! Which of you all
Will now deny to dance? She that makes dainty,
She, I'll swear, hath corns. Am I come near ye now?
Welcome, gentlemen! I have seen the day
That I have worn a visor and could tell
A whispering tale in a fair lady's ear,
Such as would please. 'Tis gone, 'tis gone, 'tis gone.
You are welcome, gentlemen! Come, musicians, play!
A hall, a hall! give room! and foot it, girls.

Music plays, and they dance

(*To the* SERVANTS) More light, you knaves; and turn the
    tables up,
And quench the fire, the room is grown too hot.

(*To himself*) Ah, sirrah, this unlooked-for sport
    comes well.
(*To his* COUSIN) Nay, sit, nay, sit, good cousin Capulet.
For you and I are past our dancing days.
How long is't now since last yourself and I
Were in a masque?

COUSIN

                  By'r lady, thirty years.

CAPULET

What, man! 'Tis not so much, 'tis not so much!
'Tis since the nuptials of Lucentio,
Come pentecost as quickly as it will,
Some five and twenty years, and then we masqued.

COUSIN

'Tis more, 'tis more, his son is elder, Sir;
His son is thirty.

CAPULET

              Will you tell me that?
His son was but a ward two years ago.
(*Watching the dancers*) Good youth i' faith. O youth's a
    jolly thing.

ROMEO

(*To a* SERVANT) What lady's that, which doth enrich the hand
Of yonder knight?

SERVANT

I know not, Sir.

ROMEO

(*To himself*) O, she doth teach the torches to burn bright!
It seems she hangs upon the cheek of night
As a rich jewel in an Ethiop's ear;
Beauty too rich for use, for earth too dear!
So shows a snowy dove trooping with crows,
As yonder lady o'er her fellows shows.
The measure done, I'll watch her place of stand,
And, touching hers, make blessèd my rude hand.
Did my heart love till now? Forswear it, sight!
For I ne'er saw true beauty till this night.

TYBALT

This, by his voice, should be a Montague.
Fetch me my rapier, boy. (*Exit Page*) What dares the slave
Come hither, covered with an antic face,
To fleer and scorn at our solemnity?
Now, by the stock and honour of my kin,
To strike him dead, I hold it not a sin.

CAPULET

Why, how now, kinsman! Wherefore storm you so?

TYBALT

Uncle, this is a Montague, our foe,
A villain that is hither come in spite,
To scorn at our solemnity this night.

CAPULET

Young Romeo is it?

TYBALT

'Tis he, that villain Romeo.

CAPULET

Content thee, gentle coz, let him alone.
'A bears him like a portly gentleman,
And, to say truth, Verona brags of him
To be a virtuous and well-governed youth.
I would not for the wealth of all the town
Here in my house do him disparagement.
Therefore be patient, take no note of him.
It is my will, the which if thou respect,
Show a fair presence and put off these frowns,
And ill-beseeming semblance for a feast.

TYBALT

It fits, when such a villain is a guest.
I'll not endure him.

CAPULET

He shall be endured.
What, goodman boy! I say, he shall. Go to!
Am I the master here, or you? Go to!
You'll not endure him! God shall mend my soul!
You'll make a mutiny among my guests!
You will set cock-a-hoop! You'll be the man!

TYBALT

Why, uncle, 'tis a shame.

CAPULET

Go to, go to!
You are a saucy boy. Is't so, indeed?
This trick may chance to scathe you, I know what.
You must contrary me! Marry, 'tis time.
(*To the dancers*) Well said, my hearts! (*To* TYBALT) You are
     a princox, go!
Be quiet, or—(*To the* SERVANTS) More light, more light!—For
     shame!
(*To* TYBALT) I'll make you quiet. (*To the dancers*) What,
     cheerly, my hearts!

DISK LINK
There's a quotation on this page that will help you play WHO SAID WHAT?

TYBALT

(*Aside*) Patience perforce with wilful choler meeting
Makes my flesh tremble in their different greeting.
I will withdraw, but this intrusion shall
Now seeming sweet, convert to bitterest gall.

Exit TYBALT

ROMEO

(*To* JULIET) If I profane with my unworthiest hand
This holy shrine, the gentle sin is this:
My lips, two blushing pilgrims, ready stand
To smooth that rough touch with a tender kiss.

JULIET

Good pilgrim, you do wrong your hand too much,
Which mannerly devotion shows in this;
For saints have hands that pilgrims' hands do touch,
And palm to palm is holy palmers' kiss.

ROMEO

Have not saints lips, and holy palmers too?

JULIET

Ay, pilgrim, lips that they must use in prayer.

ROMEO

O, then, dear saint, let lips do what hands do;
They pray, "Grant thou, lest faith turn to despair."

JULIET

Saints do not move, though grant for prayers' sake.

ROMEO

Then move not, while my prayer's effect I take.
Thus from my lips, by thine, my sin is purged.

He kisses her

JULIET

Then have my lips the sin that they have took.

ROMEO

Sin from thy lips? O trespass sweetly urged!
Give me my sin again.

He kisses her again

JULIET

You kiss by the book.

NURSE *approaches* JULIET

45

NURSE
> Madam, your mother craves a word with you.

JULIET joins her mother

ROMEO
> What is her mother?

NURSE
>   Marry, bachelor,
> Her mother is the lady of the house,
> And a good lady, and a wise and virtuous.
> I nursed her daughter, that you talked withal.
> I tell you, he that can lay hold of her
> Shall have the chinks.

ROMEO
>   Is she a Capulet?
> O dear account! My life is my foe's debt.

BENVOLIO
> Away, be gone; the sport is at the best.

ROMEO
> Ay, so I fear; the more is my unrest.

CAPULET
> Nay, gentlemen, prepare not to be gone;
> We have a trifling foolish banquet towards.

The Masked men whisper to him

> Is it e'en so? Why, then, I thank you all
> I thank you, honest gentlemen; good night.
> (*To the* SERVANTS) More torches here! Come on then,
>   let's to bed.
> (*To himself*) Ah, sirrah, by my fay, it waxes late;
> I'll to my rest.

Exeunt all but JULIET *and* NURSE

JULIET
> Come hither, Nurse. What is yond gentleman?

NURSE
> The son and heir of old Tiberio.

JULIET
> What's he that now is going out of door?

NURSE
> Marry, that, I think, be young Petrucio.

JULIET

What's he that follows there, that would not dance?

NURSE

I know not.

JULIET

Go ask his name. (*Exit* NURSE) If he be marrièd.
My grave is like to be my wedding bed.

NURSE

(*Returning*) His name is Romeo, and a Montague;
The only son of your great enemy.

JULIET

(*Aside*) My only love sprung from my only hate!
Too early seen unknown, and known too late!
Prodigious birth of love it is to me,
That I must love a loathèd enemy.

NURSE

What's this? what's this?

JULIET

A rhyme I learnt even now
Of one I danced withal.

LADY CAPULET *calls* JULIET *from within*

NURSE

Anon, anon!
Come, let's away; the strangers all are gone.

Exeunt

PROLOGUE

Enter CHORUS

PROLOGUE TO ACT 2
THE CHORUS REMINDS US OF WHAT
HAS HAPPENED SO FAR.

CHORUS
Now old desire doth in his death-bed lie,
    And young affection gapes to be his heir;
That fair for which love groaned for and would die,
    With tender Juliet matched, is now not fair.
Now Romeo is beloved and loves again,
    Alike bewitchèd by the charm of looks,
But to his foe supposed he must complain,
    And she steal love's sweet bait from fearful hooks;
Being held a foe, he may not have access
    To breathe such vows as lovers use to swear,
And she as much in love, her means much less
    To meet her new belovèd anywhere;
But passion lends them power, time means, to meet,
    Tempering extremities with extreme sweet.

Exit

SCENE 1
A street by the wall of Capulet's orchard

ACT 2 SCENE 1
AFTER THE PARTY, ROMEO HIDES
FROM HIS FRIENDS DESPITE HEARING
MERCUTIO'S JOKES ABOUT HIS LOVE
FOR ROSALINE. WE ALREADY KNOW
THAT HE DOES NOT LOVE ROSALINE
ANY MORE, BUT JULIET.

Enter ROMEO

ROMEO
Can I go forward when my heart is here?
Turn back, dull earth, and find thy centre out.

He climbs the wall, and jumps down into the orchard behind it.
Enter BENVOLIO *and* MERCUTIO *into the street.* ROMEO *listens*
from the orchard

BENVOLIO
Romeo! My cousin Romeo! Romeo!
MERCUTIO
                                        He is wise,
And, on my life, hath stolen him home to bed.
BENVOLIO
He ran this way, and leapt this orchard wall.
Call, good Mercutio.

MERCUTIO

                 Nay, I'll conjure too.
Romeo! Humours! Madman! Passion! Liver!
Appear thou in the likeness of a sigh;
Speak but one rhyme, and I am satisfied;
Cry but "Ay me!" pronounce but "love" and "dove;"
Speak to my gossip Venus one fair word,
One nickname for her purblind son and heir,
Young Abraham Cupid, he that shot so trim,
When King Cophetua loved the beggar-maid!
He heareth not, he stirreth not, he moveth not;
The ape is dead, and I must conjure him.
(*Addressing* ROMEO) I conjure thee by Rosaline's bright eyes,
By her high forehead and her scarlet lip,
By her fine foot, straight leg and quivering thigh
And the demesnes that there adjacent lie,
That in thy likeness thou appear to us!

BENVOLIO

And if he hear thee, thou wilt anger him.

MERCUTIO

This cannot anger him. 'Twould anger him
To raise a spirit in his mistress' circle
Of some strange nature, letting it there stand
Till she had laid it and conjured it down.
That were some spite. My invocation
Is fair and honest, and in his mistress' name
I conjure only but to raise up him.

BENVOLIO

Come, he hath hid himself among these trees,
To be consorted with the humorous night.
Blind is his love and best befits the dark.

MERCUTIO

If love be blind, love cannot hit the mark.
Now will he sit under a medlar tree,
And wish his mistress were that kind of fruit
As maids call medlars, when they laugh alone.
O Romeo, that she were, O that she were
An open etcetera, thou a Poperin pear!
Romeo, good night. I'll to my truckle-bed;
This field-bed is too cold for me to sleep.
Come, shall we go?

BENVOLIO

             Go, then; for 'tis in vain
To seek him here that means not to be found.

Exeunt

2.2

ACT 2 SCENE 2

ROMEO HIDES IN THE CAPULET ORCHARD AND SEES JULIET ON HER BALCONY. SHE DOESN'T KNOW THAT ROMEO IS THERE, AND DECLARES HER LOVE FOR HIM. WHEN ROMEO SPEAKS TO HER, SHE IS EMBARRASSED. SOON, THOUGH, THEY MAKE PROMISES TO EACH OTHER OF LOVE AND MARRIAGE.

DISK LINK

Can you remember all the characters, props, and sound effects in this scene? Test yourself in MAKE A SCENE.

SCENE 2
Capulet's orchard

Enter ROMEO

ROMEO
He jests at scars that never felt a wound.

JULIET *appears above at a window*

But, soft! What light through yonder window breaks?
It is the east, and Juliet is the sun.
Arise, fair sun, and kill the envious moon,
Who is already sick and pale with grief,
That thou her maid art far more fair than she.
Be not her maid, since she is envious.
Her vestal livery is but sick and green
And none but fools do wear it. Cast it off.
It is my lady, O, it is my love!
O, that she knew she were!
She speaks yet she says nothing. What of that?
Her eye discourses; I will answer it.
I am too bold; 'tis not to me she speaks.
Two of the fairest stars in all the heaven,
Having some business, do entreat her eyes
To twinkle in their spheres till they return.
What if her eyes were there, they in her head?
The brightness of her cheek would shame those stars
As daylight doth a lamp; her eyes in heaven
Would through the airy region stream so bright
That birds would sing and think it were not night.
See how she leans her cheek upon her hand!
O, that I were a glove upon that hand,
That I might touch that cheek!

JULIET
                    Ay me!

ROMEO
                         She speaks.
O, speak again, bright angel! For thou art
As glorious to this night, being o'er my head,
As is a wingèd messenger of heaven
Unto the white-upturnèd wondering eyes
Of mortals that fall back to gaze on him

When he bestrides the lazy-pacing clouds
And sails upon the bosom of the air.

JULIET

O Romeo, Romeo! Wherefore art thou Romeo?
Deny thy father and refuse thy name!
Or, if thou wilt not, be but sworn my love,
And I'll no longer be a Capulet.

ROMEO

(*Aside*) Shall I hear more, or shall I speak at this?

JULIET

'Tis but thy name that is my enemy.
Thou art thyself, though not a Montague.
What's "Montague?" It is nor hand, nor foot,
Nor arm, nor face, nor any other part
Belonging to a man. O, be some other name!
What's in a name? That which we call a rose
By any other name would smell as sweet.
So Romeo would, were he not Romeo called,
Retain that dear perfection which he owes
Without that title. Romeo, doff thy name,
And for that name which is no part of thee
Take all myself.

ROMEO

    (*To* JULIET) I take thee at thy word.
Call me but "Love," and I'll be new baptised;
Henceforth I never will be Romeo.

JULIET

What man art thou that thus bescreened in night
So stumblest on my counsel?

ROMEO

                     By a name
I know not how to tell thee who I am.
My name, dear saint, is hateful to myself,
Because it is an enemy to thee.
Had I it written, I would tear the word.

JULIET

My ears have not yet drunk a hundred words
Of that tongue's utterance, yet I know the sound.
Art thou not Romeo and a Montague?

ROMEO

Neither, fair maid, if either thee dislike.

JULIET

How camest thou hither, tell me, and wherefore?
The orchard walls are high and hard to climb,

And the place death, considering who thou art,
If any of my kinsmen find thee here.

ROMEO

With love's light wings did I o'erperch these walls;
For stony limits cannot hold love out,
And what love can do that dares love attempt.
Therefore thy kinsmen are no stop to me.

JULIET

If they do see thee, they will murder thee.

ROMEO

Alack, there lies more peril in thine eye
Than twenty of their swords! Look thou but sweet,
And I am proof against their enmity.

JULIET

I would not for the world they saw thee here.

ROMEO

I have night's cloak to hide me from their eyes;
And but thou love me, let them find me here.
My life were better ended by their hate,
Than death proroguèd, wanting of thy love.

JULIET

By whose direction found'st thou out this place?

ROMEO

By love, that first did prompt me to inquire.
He lent me counsel and I lent him eyes.
I am no pilot; yet, wert thou as far
As that vast shore washed with the farthest sea,
I would adventure for such merchandise.

JULIET

Thou know'st the mask of night is on my face,
Else would a maiden blush bepaint my cheek
For that which thou hast heard me speak tonight
Fain would I dwell on form; fain, fain deny
What I have spoke: but farewell compliment!
Dost thou love me? I know thou wilt say "Ay,"
And I will take thy word. Yet if thou swear'st,
Thou mayst prove false. At lovers' perjuries
They say, Jove laughs. O gentle Romeo,
If thou dost love, pronounce it faithfully.
Or if thou think'st I am too quickly won,
I'll frown and be perverse and say thee nay,
So thou wilt woo; but else, not for the world.
In truth, fair Montague, I am too fond,
And therefore thou mayst think my 'haviour light;

But trust me, gentleman, I'll prove more true
Than those that have more cunning to be strange.
I should have been more strange, I must confess,
But that thou overheard'st, ere I was ware,
My true love's passion. Therefore pardon me,
And not impute this yielding to light love,
Which the dark night hath so discoverèd.

ROMEO

Lady, by yonder blessèd moon I vow
That tips with silver all these fruit-tree tops—

JULIET

O, swear not by the moon, th' inconstant moon,
That monthly changes in her circled orb,
Lest that thy love prove likewise variable.

ROMEO

What shall I swear by?

JULIET

               Do not swear at all;
Or, if thou wilt, swear by thy gracious self,
Which is the god of my idolatry,
And I'll believe thee.

ROMEO

             If my heart's dear love—

JULIET

Well, do not swear. Although I joy in thee,
I have no joy of this contract tonight.
It is too rash, too unadvised, too sudden;
Too like the lightning, which doth cease to be
Ere one can say, "it lightens." Sweet, good night!
This bud of love, by summer's ripening breath,
May prove a beauteous flower when next we meet.
Good night, good night! As sweet repose and rest
Come to thy heart as that within my breast!

ROMEO

O, wilt thou leave me so unsatisfied?

JULIET

What satisfaction canst thou have tonight?

ROMEO

Th' exchange of thy love's faithful vow for mine.

JULIET

I gave thee mine before thou didst request it;
And yet I would it were to give again.

ROMEO

Wouldst thou withdraw it? For what purpose, love?

DISK LINK
There's a quotation on this page that will help you play WHO SAID WHAT?

JULIET
But to be frank, and give it thee again.
And yet I wish but for the thing I have.
My bounty is as boundless as the sea,
My love as deep; the more I give to thee,
The more I have, for both are infinite.

NURSE *calls within*

I hear some noise within. Dear love, adieu!
(*To* NURSE) Anon, good Nurse! (*To* ROMEO) Sweet
    Montague, be true.
Stay but a little, I will come again.

Exit JULIET, *above*

ROMEO
O blessed, blessed night! I am afeard,
Being in night, all this is but a dream,
Too flattering-sweet to be substantial.

Re-enter JULIET, *above*

JULIET
Three words, dear Romeo, and good night indeed.
If that thy bent of love be honourable,
Thy purpose marriage, send me word tomorrow,
By one that I'll procure to come to thee,
Where and what time thou wilt perform the rite;
And all my fortunes at thy foot I'll lay
And follow thee, my lord, throughout the world.

NURSE
(*Within*) Madam!

JULIET
I come, anon. (*To* ROMEO) But if thou mean'st not well,
I do beseech thee—

NURSE
(*Within*) Madam!

JULIET
                    By and by, I come—
(*To* ROMEO) To cease thy suit, and leave me to my grief.
Tomorrow will I send.

ROMEO
                    So thrive my soul—

JULIET

A thousand times good night!

Exit JULIET, *above*

ROMEO

A thousand times the worse, to want thy light!
Love goes toward love, as schoolboys from their books,
But love from love, toward school with heavy looks.

ROMEO *is about to leave as* JULIET *returns*

JULIET

Hist! Romeo, hist! O, for a falconer's voice,
To lure this tassel-gentle back again!
Bondage is hoarse and may not speak aloud;
Else would I tear the cave where Echo lies,
And make her airy tongue more hoarse than mine
With repetition of my Romeo's name.

ROMEO

It is my soul that calls upon my name.
How silver-sweet sound lovers' tongues by night,
Like softest music to attending ears!

JULIET

Romeo!

ROMEO

              My dear?

JULIET

                              What o'clock tomorrow
Shall I send to thee?

ROMEO

                              By the hour of nine.

JULIET

I will not fail. 'Tis twenty years till then.
I have forgot why I did call thee back.

ROMEO

Let me stand here till thou remember it.

JULIET

I shall forget, to have thee still stand there,
Remembering how I love thy company.

ROMEO

And I'll still stay, to have thee still forget,
Forgetting any other home but this.

JULIET

'Tis almost morning. I would have thee gone—

And yet no farther than a wanton's bird,
Who lets it hop a little from her hand,
Like a poor prisoner in his twisted gyves,
And with a silk thread plucks it back again,
So loving-jealous of his liberty.

ROMEO

I would I were thy bird.

JULIET

                        Sweet, so would I.
Yet I should kill thee with much cherishing.
Good night, good night! Parting is such sweet sorrow,
That I shall say "good night" till it be morrow.

Exit JULIET *above*

ROMEO

Sleep dwell upon thine eyes, peace in thy breast!
Would I were sleep and peace, so sweet to rest!
Hence will I to my ghostly sire's close cell,
His help to crave, and my dear hap to tell.

Exit

ACT 2 SCENE 3
ROMEO ASKS FRIAR LAWRENCE IF HE WILL AGREE TO MARRY THE LOVERS. THE FRIAR IS RELUCTANT AT FIRST, BUT SEES IT AS AN OPPORTUNITY TO BRING THE TWO FAMILIES TOGETHER. HE AGREES TO PERFORM THE CEREMONY.

SCENE 3

Friar Lawrence's cell

Enter FRIAR LAWRENCE, *with a basket*

FRIAR LAWRENCE

The grey-eyed morn smiles on the frowning night,
Chequering the eastern clouds with streaks of light,
And fleckled darkness like a drunkard reels
From forth day's path and Titan's fiery wheels.
Now, ere the sun advance his burning eye
The day to cheer and night's dank dew to dry,
I must up-fill this osier cage of ours
With baleful weeds and precious-juicèd flowers.
The earth that's nature's mother is her tomb.
What is her burying grave that is her womb,
And from her womb children of divers kind
We sucking on her natural bosom find;
Many for many virtues excellent,
None but for some and yet all different.
O, mickle is the powerful grace that lies

DISK LINK
Guess what Shakespeare's more difficult words and phrases mean in the GLOSSARY GAME.

In plants, herbs, stones, and their true qualities;
For nought so vile that on the earth doth live
But to the earth some special good doth give;
Nor aught so good but strained from that fair use
Revolts from true birth, stumbling on abuse.
Virtue itself turns vice, being misapplied,
And vice sometimes by action dignified.
Within the infant rind of this weak flower
Poison hath residence and medicine power;
For this, being smelt, with that part cheers each part;
Being tasted, stays all senses with the heart.
Two such opposèd kings encamp them still
In man as well as herbs—grace and rude will;
And where the worser is predominant,
Full soon the canker death eats up that plant.

Enter ROMEO

ROMEO
Good morrow, father.

FRIAR LAWRENCE
                    Benedicite!
What early tongue so sweet saluteth me?
Young son, it argues a distempered head
So soon to bid good morrow to thy bed.
Care keeps his watch in every old man's eye,
And where care lodges, sleep will never lie;
But where unbruisèd youth with unstuffed brain
Doth couch his limbs, there golden sleep doth reign.
Therefore thy earliness doth me assure
Thou art up-roused by some distemperature;
Or if not so, then here I hit it right,
Our Romeo hath not been in bed tonight.

ROMEO
That last is true; the sweeter rest was mine.

FRIAR LAWRENCE
God pardon sin! Wast thou with Rosaline?

ROMEO
With Rosaline, my ghostly father? No.
I have forgot that name, and that name's woe.

FRIAR LAWRENCE
That's my good son! But where hast thou been, then?

ROMEO
I'll tell thee, ere thou ask it me again.

I have been feasting with mine enemy,
Where on a sudden one hath wounded me,
That's by me wounded. Both our remedies
Within thy help and holy physic lies.
I bear no hatred, blessed man, for, lo,
My intercession likewise steads my foe.

FRIAR LAWRENCE

Be plain, good son, and homely in thy drift.
Riddling confession finds but riddling shrift.

ROMEO

Then plainly know my heart's dear love is set
On the fair daughter of rich Capulet;
As mine on hers, so hers is set on mine,
And all combined, save what thou must combine
By holy marriage. When, and where, and how
We met, we wooed and made exchange of vow,
I'll tell thee as we pass; but this I pray,
That thou consent to marry us today.

FRIAR LAWRENCE

Holy Saint Francis, what a change is here!
Is Rosaline, whom thou didst love so dear,
So soon forsaken? Young men's love then lies
Not truly in their hearts, but in their eyes.
Jesu Maria, what a deal of brine
Hath washed thy sallow cheeks for Rosaline!
How much salt water thrown away in waste,
To season love, that of it doth not taste!
The sun not yet thy sighs from heaven clears,
Thy old groans ring yet in my ancient ears.
Lo, here upon thy cheek the stain doth sit
Of an old tear that is not washed off yet.
If e'er thou wast thyself and these woes thine,
Thou and these woes were all for Rosaline.
And art thou changed? Pronounce this sentence then:
Women may fall, when there's no strength in men.

ROMEO

Thou chid'st me oft for loving Rosaline.

FRIAR LAWRENCE

For doting, not for loving, pupil mine.

ROMEO

And bad'st me bury love.

FRIAR LAWRENCE

       Not in a grave,
To lay one in, another out to have.

ROMEO

I pray thee, chide me not. Her I love now
Doth grace for grace and love for love allow.
The other did not so.

FRIAR LAWRENCE

O, she knew well
Thy love did read by rote and could not spell.
But come, young waverer, come, go with me,
In one respect I'll thy assistant be;
For this alliance may so happy prove,
To turn your households' rancour to pure love.

ROMEO

O, let us hence! I stand on sudden haste.

FRIAR LAWRENCE

Wisely, and slow. They stumble that run fast.

Exeunt

SCENE 4
A street in Verona

Enter BENVOLIO *and* MERCUTIO

MERCUTIO

Where the devil should this Romeo be? Came he
not home tonight?

BENVOLIO

Not to his father's. I spoke with his man.

MERCUTIO

Why, that same pale hard-hearted wench, that Rosaline,
torments him so, that he will sure run mad.

BENVOLIO

Tybalt, the kinsman of old Capulet, hath sent a letter to
his father's house.

MERCUTIO

A challenge, on my life.

BENVOLIO

Romeo will answer it.

MERCUTIO

Any man that can write may answer a letter.

BENVOLIO

Nay, he will answer the letter's master, how he dares,
being dared.

DISK LINK
Test your knowledge of the play in WALK-THROUGH ROMEO AND JULIET. This quiz will sort the swans from the crows!

MERCUTIO

Alas, poor Romeo, he is already dead! Stabbed with a white wench's black eye; run through the ear with a love song; the very pin of his heart cleft with the blind bow-boy's butt-shaft; and is he a man to encounter Tybalt?

BENVOLIO

Why, what is Tybalt?

MERCUTIO

More than Prince of Cats, I can tell you. O, he is the courageous captain of compliments. He fights as you sing prick-song, keeps time, distance, and proportion; he rests me his minim rests, one, two, and the third in your bosom! The very butcher of a silk button, a duellist, a duellist; a gentleman of the very first house, of the first and second cause. Ah, the immortal passado! the punto reverso! the hai!

BENVOLIO

The what?

MERCUTIO

The pox of such antic, lisping, affecting fantasticoes, these new tuners of accents! "By Jesu, a very good blade! A very tall man! A very good whore!" Why, is not this a lamentable thing, grandsire, that we should be thus afflicted with these strange flies, these fashion-mongers, these "pardon-me's," who stand so much on the new form that they cannot sit at ease on the old bench? O, their bones, their bones!

Enter ROMEO

BENVOLIO

Here comes Romeo! Here comes Romeo!

MERCUTIO

Without his roe, like a dried herring. O, flesh, flesh, how art thou fishified! Now is he for the numbers that Petrarch flowed in. Laura to his lady was a kitchen wench (marry, she had a better love to berhyme her) Dido a dowdy, Cleopatra a gipsy, Helen and Hero hildings and harlots, Thisbe a grey eye or so, but not to the purpose. Signior Romeo, bonjour! There's a French salutation to your French slop. You gave us the counterfeit fairly last night.

ROMEO

Good morrow to you both. What counterfeit did I give you?

MERCUTIO

The slip, Sir, the slip. Can you not conceive?

ROMEO
Pardon, good Mercutio. My business was great, and in such a case as mine a man may strain courtesy.

MERCUTIO
That's as much as to say, such a case as yours constrains a man to bow in the hams.

ROMEO
Meaning, to curtsy?

MERCUTIO
Thou hast most kindly hit it.

ROMEO
A most courteous exposition.

MERCUTIO
Nay, I am the very pink of courtesy.

ROMEO
Pink for flower?

MERCUTIO
Right.

ROMEO
Why, then is my pump well flowered.

MERCUTIO
Sure wit! Follow me this jest now till thou hast worn out thy pump, that when the single sole of it is worn, the jest may remain after the wearing, solely singular.

ROMEO
O single-soled jest, solely singular for the singleness!

MERCUTIO
Come between us, good Benvolio! My wits faints.

ROMEO
Switch and spurs, switch and spurs! Or I'll cry a match.

MERCUTIO
Nay, if our wits run the wild-goose chase, I am done; for thou hast more of the wild-goose in one of thy wits than, I am sure, I have in my whole five. Was I with you there for the goose?

ROMEO
Thou wast never with me for anything when thou wast not there for the goose.

MERCUTIO
I will bite thee by the ear for that jest.

ROMEO
Nay, good goose, bite not.

MERCUTIO
Thy wit is a very bitter sweeting; it is a most sharp sauce.

ROMEO

And is it not well served in to a sweet goose?

MERCUTIO

O here's a wit of cheveril, that stretches from an inch narrow to an ell broad!

ROMEO

I stretch it out for that word "broad" which, added to the "goose," proves thee far and wide a broad goose.

MERCUTIO

Why, is not this better now than groaning for love? Now art thou sociable; now art thou Romeo; now art thou what thou art, by art as well as by nature. For this drivelling love is like a great natural, that runs lolling up and down to hide his bauble in a hole.

BENVOLIO

Stop there, stop there.

MERCUTIO

Thou desirest me to stop in my tale against the hair.

BENVOLIO

Thou wouldst else have made thy tale large.

MERCUTIO

O, thou art deceived; I would have made it short, for I was come to the whole depth of my tale, and meant, indeed, to occupy the argument no longer.

Enter NURSE *and her servant* PETER

ROMEO

Here's goodly gear! A sail, a sail!

MERCUTIO

Two, two; a shirt and a smock.

NURSE

Peter!

PETER

Anon!

NURSE

My fan, Peter.

MERCUTIO

Good Peter, to hide her face; for her fan's the fairer face.

NURSE

God ye good morrow, gentlemen.

MERCUTIO

God ye good e'en, fair gentlewoman.

NURSE

Is it good e'en?

MERCUTIO

'Tis no less, I tell you, for the bawdy hand of the dial is now
upon the prick of noon.

NURSE

Out upon you! What a man are you!

ROMEO

One, gentlewoman, that God hath made for himself to mar.

NURSE

By my troth, it is well said, "for himself to mar," quoth 'a?
Gentlemen, can any of you tell me where I may find the
young Romeo?

ROMEO

I can tell you; but young Romeo will be older when you
have found him than he was when you sought him. I am
the youngest of that name, for fault of a worse.

NURSE

You say well.

MERCUTIO

Yea, is the worst well? Very well took, i' faith; wisely, wisely.

NURSE

If you be he, Sir, I desire some confidence with you.

BENVOLIO

She will indite him to some supper.

MERCUTIO

A bawd, a bawd, a bawd! So ho!

ROMEO

What hast thou found?

MERCUTIO

No hare, Sir; unless a hare, Sir, in a lenten pie,
that is something stale and hoar ere it be spent.

He sings

> An old hare hoar,
> And an old hare hoar,
> Is very good meat in Lent.
> But a hare that is hoar
> Is too much for a score,
> When it hoars ere it be spent.

Romeo, will you come to your father's? We'll to
dinner, thither.

DISK LINK
Guess what Shakespeare's more difficult words and phrases mean in the GLOSSARY GAME.

ROMEO

I will follow you.

MERCUTIO

Farewell, ancient lady; farewell,

Singing

Lady, lady, lady.

Exeunt MERCUTIO *and* BENVOLIO

NURSE

I pray you, Sir, what saucy merchant was this, that was so full of his ropery?

ROMEO

A gentleman, Nurse, that loves to hear himself talk, and will speak more in a minute than he will stand to in a month.

NURSE

And 'a speak anything against me, I'll take him down, and 'a were lustier than he is, and twenty such Jacks; and if I cannot, I'll find those that shall. Scurvy knave! I am none of his flirt-gills; I am none of his skains-mates. (*To* PETER) And thou must stand by too, and suffer every knave to use me at his pleasure?

PETER

I saw no man use you at his pleasure. If I had, my weapon should quickly have been out, I warrant you. I dare draw as soon as another man, if I see occasion in a good quarrel, and the law on my side.

NURSE

Now, afore God, I am so vexed, that every part about me quivers. (*Referring to* MERCUTIO) Scurvy knave! (*To* ROMEO) Pray you, Sir, a word; and as I told you, my young lady bid me inquire you out. What she bid me say, I will keep to myself; but first let me tell ye, if ye should lead her into a fool's paradise, as they say, it were a very gross kind of behaviour, as they say, for the gentlewoman is young; and, therefore, if you should deal double with her, truly it were an ill thing to be offered to any gentlewoman, and very weak dealing.

ROMEO

Nurse, commend me to thy lady and mistress. I protest unto thee—

NURSE

Good heart, and, i' faith, I will tell her as much.

Lord, Lord, she will be a joyful woman.

ROMEO

What wilt thou tell her, Nurse? Thou dost not mark me.

NURSE

I will tell her, Sir, that you do protest; which, as I take it, is a gentlemanlike offer.

ROMEO

                             Bid her devise
Some means to come to shrift this afternoon;
And there she shall at Friar Lawrence's cell
Be shrived and married. (*He offers her money*) Here is for
    thy pains.

NURSE

No truly Sir; not a penny.

ROMEO

Go to; I say you shall.

NURSE

(*Taking the money*) This afternoon, Sir? Well, she shall
    be there.

ROMEO

And stay, good Nurse, behind the abbey wall.
Within this hour my man shall be with thee
And bring thee cords made like a tackled stair,
Which to the high top-gallant of my joy
Must be my convoy in the secret night.
Farewell! Be trusty, and I'll quit thy pains.
Farewell! Commend me to thy mistress.

NURSE

Now God in heaven bless thee! Hark you, Sir.

ROMEO

What say'st thou, my dear Nurse?

NURSE

Is your man secret? Did you ne'er hear say,
"Two may keep counsel, putting one away?"

ROMEO

I warrant thee, my man's as true as steel.

NURSE

Well, Sir; my mistress is the sweetest lady. Lord, Lord!
When 'twas a little prating thing—O, there is a nobleman in
town, one Paris, that would fain lay knife aboard; but she,
good soul, had as lief see a toad, a very toad, as see him. I
anger her sometimes and tell her that Paris is the properer
man; but, I'll warrant you, when I say so, she looks as pale as
any clout in the versal world. Doth not "rosemary" and

"Romeo" begin both with a letter?

ROMEO

Ay, Nurse, what of that? Both with an "R."

NURSE

Ah, mocker! That's the dog's name; "R" is for the—No; I know it begins with some other letter—and she hath the prettiest sententious of it, of you and rosemary, that it would do you good to hear it.

ROMEO

Commend me to thy lady.

NURSE

Ay, a thousand times.

Exit ROMEO

Peter!

PETER

Anon!

NURSE

Peter, take my fan, and go before and apace.

Exeunt

ACT 2 SCENE 5
JULIET IS WAITING ANXIOUSLY FOR NURSE TO RETURN WITH NEWS OF ROMEO. WHEN SHE DOES SHE TEASES JULIET, MAKING HER WAIT BEFORE SHE WILL TELL HER THE GOOD NEWS.

SCENE 5
Capulet's orchard

Enter JULIET

JULIET

The clock struck nine when I did send the Nurse;
In half an hour she promised to return.
Perchance she cannot meet him. That's not so.
O, she is lame! Love's heralds should be thoughts,
Which ten times faster glide than the sun's beams,
Driving back shadows over louring hills.
Therefore do nimble-pinioned doves draw love,
And therefore hath the wind-swift Cupid wings.
Now is the sun upon the highmost hill
Of this day's journey, and from nine till twelve
Is three long hours, yet she is not come.
Had she affections and warm youthful blood,
She would be as swift in motion as a ball;
My words would bandy her to my sweet love,
And his to me.

But old folks, many feign as they were dead—
Unwieldy, slow, heavy and pale as lead.

Enter NURSE *and* PETER

O God, she comes! O honey Nurse, what news?
Hast thou met with him? Send thy man away.

NURSE
Peter, stay at the gate.

Exit PETER

JULIET
Now, good sweet Nurse—O Lord, why lookest thou sad?
Though news be sad, yet tell them merrily;
If good, thou shamest the music of sweet news
By playing it to me with so sour a face.

NURSE
I am aweary, give me leave awhile.
Fie, how my bones ache! What a jaunt have I had!

JULIET
I would thou hadst my bones, and I thy news.
Nay, come, I pray thee, speak; good, good Nurse, speak.

NURSE
Jesu, what haste? Can you not stay awhile?
Do you not see that I am out of breath?

JULIET
How art thou out of breath, when thou hast breath
To say to me that thou art out of breath?
The excuse that thou dost make in this delay
Is longer than the tale thou dost excuse.
Is thy news good, or bad? Answer to that;
Say either, and I'll stay the circumstance.
Let me be satisfied, is't good or bad?

NURSE
Well, you have made a simple choice; you know not how
to choose a man. Romeo? No, not he. Though his face be
better than any man's, yet his leg excels all men's; and for
a hand, and a foot, and a body, though they be not to be
talked on, yet they are past compare. He is not the flower
of courtesy, but, I'll warrant him, as gentle as a lamb. Go thy
ways, wench; serve God. What, have you dined at home?

JULIET
No, no. But all this did I know before.
What says he of our marriage? What of that?

NURSE

Lord, how my head aches! What a head have I!
It beats as it would fall in twenty pieces.
My back o' t'other side—O, my back, my back!
Beshrew your heart for sending me about,
To catch my death with jaunting up and down!

JULIET

I' faith, I am sorry that thou art not well.
Sweet, sweet, sweet Nurse, tell me, what says my love?

NURSE

Your love says, like an honest gentleman, and a courteous,
and a kind, and a handsome, and, I warrant, a virtuous—
Where is your mother?

JULIET

Where is my mother? Why, she is within;
Where should she be? How oddly thou repliest!
"Your love says, like an honest gentleman,
'Where is your mother?'"

NURSE

                              O God's lady dear!
Are you so hot? Marry, come up, I trow;
Is this the poultice for my aching bones?
Henceforward do your messages yourself.

JULIET

Here's such a coil! Come, what says Romeo?

NURSE

Have you got leave to go to shrift today?

JULIET

I have.

NURSE

Then hie you hence to Friar Lawrence's cell;
There stays a husband to make you a wife.
Now comes the wanton blood up in your cheeks,
They'll be in scarlet straight at any news.
Hie you to church; I must another way,
To fetch a ladder, by the which your love
Must climb a bird's nest soon when it is dark.
I am the drudge and toil in your delight,
But you shall bear the burden soon at night.
Go—I'll to dinner: hie you to the cell.

JULIET

Hie to high fortune! Honest Nurse, farewell.

Exeunt

ACT 2 SCENE 6
ROMEO AND JULIET MEET AT THE
FRIAR'S CELL AND THEN GO TO THE
CHURCH TO BE MARRIED.

DISK LINK
There's a quotation on this
page that will help you play
WHO SAID WHAT?

SCENE 6
Friar Lawrence's cell

Enter FRIAR LAWRENCE *and* ROMEO

FRIAR LAWRENCE
So smile the heavens upon this holy act,
That after hours with sorrow chide us not!
ROMEO
Amen, amen! But come what sorrow can,
It cannot countervail the exchange of joy
That one short minute gives me in her sight.
Do thou but close our hands with holy words,
Then love-devouring death do what he dare;
It is enough I may but call her mine.
FRIAR LAWRENCE
These violent delights have violent ends
And in their triumph die like fire and powder,
Which, as they kiss, consume. The sweetest honey
Is loathsome in his own deliciousness
And in the taste confounds the appetite.
Therefore love moderately; long love doth so:
Too swift arrives as tardy as too slow.

Enter JULIET

Here comes the lady. O, so light a foot
Will ne'er wear out the everlasting flint.
A lover may bestride the gossamers
That idles in the wanton summer air,
And yet not fall, so light is vanity.
JULIET
Good even to my ghostly confessor.
FRIAR LAWRENCE
Romeo shall thank thee, daughter, for us both.

ROMEO *kisses her*

JULIET
As much to him, else is his thanks too much.

JULIET *kisses* ROMEO

ROMEO

    Ah, Juliet, if the measure of thy joy
    Be heaped like mine and that thy skill be more
    To blazon it, then sweeten with thy breath
    This neighbour air, and let rich music's tongue
    Unfold the imagined happiness that both
    Receive in either by this dear encounter.

JULIET

    Conceit, more rich in matter than in words,
    Brags of his substance, not of ornament.
    They are but beggars that can count their worth;
    But my true love is grown to such excess
    I cannot sum up sum of half my wealth.

FRIAR LAWRENCE

    Come, come with me, and we will make short work;
    For, by your leaves, you shall not stay alone
    Till holy church incorporate two in one.

Exeunt

ACT 3

SCENE 1
A street in Verona

ACT 3 SCENE 1
TYBALT TRIES TO PROVOKE ROMEO INTO A FIGHT BUT ROMEO REFUSES. ANGRY THAT ROMEO IS PUTTING UP WITH TYBALT'S INSULTS, MERCUTIO STEPS IN FOR HIM. TYBALT KILLS MERCUTIO, THEN ROMEO MURDERS TYBALT. THE PRINCE OF VERONA BANISHES ROMEO FROM THE CITY.

DISK LINK
Can you remember all the characters, props, and sound effects in this scene? Test yourself in MAKE A SCENE.

Enter MERCUTIO, BENVOLIO, *Page, and Servants*

BENVOLIO
I pray thee, good Mercutio, let's retire.
The day is hot, the Capulets are abroad,
And, if we meet, we shall not scape a brawl,
For now, these hot days, is the mad blood stirring.

MERCUTIO
Thou art like one of those fellows that, when he enters the confines of a tavern, claps me his sword upon the table and says, "God send me no need of thee;" and by the operation of the second cup draws him on the drawer, when indeed there is no need.

BENVOLIO
Am I like such a fellow?

MERCUTIO
Come, come, thou art as hot a Jack in thy mood as any in Italy, and as soon moved to be moody, and as soon moody to be moved.

BENVOLIO
And what to?

MERCUTIO
Nay, and there were two such, we should have none shortly, for one would kill the other. Thou! Why, thou wilt quarrel with a man that hath a hair more, or a hair less in his beard, than thou hast. Thou wilt quarrel with a man for cracking nuts, having no other reason but because thou hast hazel eyes. What eye but such an eye would spy out such a quarrel? Thy head is as full of quarrels as an egg is full of meat, and yet thy head hath been beaten as addle as an egg for quarrelling. Thou hast quarrelled with a man for coughing in the street, because he hath wakened thy dog that hath lain asleep in the sun. Didst thou not fall out with a tailor for wearing his new doublet before Easter? With another, for tying his new shoes with old riband? And yet thou wilt tutor me from quarrelling!

BENVOLIO
And I were so apt to quarrel as thou art, any man should buy the fee-simple of my life for an hour and a quarter.

MERCUTIO
The fee-simple! O simple!

Enter TYBALT *and others*

BENVOLIO
By my head, here come the Capulets.
MERCUTIO
By my heel, I care not.
TYBALT
(*To his companions*) Follow me close, for I will speak to
them. (*To* MERCUTIO *and* BENVOLIO) Gentlemen, good e'en.
A word with one of you.
MERCUTIO
And but one word with one of us? Couple it with
something; make it a word and a blow.
TYBALT
You shall find me apt enough to that, Sir, and you
will give me occasion.
MERCUTIO
Could you not take some occasion without giving?
TYBALT
Mercutio, thou consortest with Romeo—
MERCUTIO
Consort! What, dost thou make us minstrels? And thou
make minstrels of us, look to hear nothing but discords.
Here's my fiddlestick; here's that shall make you dance.
'Zounds, consort!
BENVOLIO
We talk here in the public haunt of men.
Either withdraw unto some private place,
Or reason coldly of your grievances,
Or else depart. Here all eyes gaze on us.
MERCUTIO
Men's eyes were made to look, and let them gaze.
I will not budge for no man's pleasure, I.

Enter ROMEO

TYBALT
(*To* MERCUTIO) Well, peace be with you, Sir. Here comes
my man.
MERCUTIO
But I'll be hanged, Sir, if he wear your livery.

Marry, go before to field, he'll be your follower;
Your worship in that sense may call him "man."

TYBALT

Romeo, the love I bear thee can afford
No better term than this—thou art a villain.

ROMEO

Tybalt, the reason that I have to love thee
Doth much excuse the appertaining rage
To such a greeting. Villain am I none.
Therefore farewell; I see thou know'st me not.

TYBALT

Boy, this shall not excuse the injuries
That thou hast done me; therefore turn and draw.

ROMEO

I do protest, I never injured thee,
But love thee better than thou canst devise,
Till thou shalt know the reason of my love:
And so, good Capulet, which name I tender
As dearly as my own, be satisfied.

MERCUTIO

O calm, dishonourable, vile submission!
Alla stoccata carries it away.

Draws his sword

Tybalt, you rat-catcher, will you walk?

TYBALT

What wouldst thou have with me?

MERCUTIO

Good King of Cats, nothing but one of your nine lives,
that I mean to make bold withal, and, as you shall use me
hereafter, dry-beat the rest of the eight. Will you pluck your
sword out of his pilcher by the ears? Make haste, lest mine
be about your ears ere it be out.

TYBALT

(*Drawing his sword*) I am for you.

ROMEO

Gentle Mercutio, put thy rapier up.

MERCUTIO

(*To* TYBALT) Come, Sir, your passado.

MERCUTIO *and* TYBALT *fight*

ROMEO

Draw, Benvolio; beat down their weapons.
Gentlemen, for shame, forbear this outrage!
Tybalt, Mercutio, the Prince expressly hath
Forbid this bandying in Verona streets.
Hold, Tybalt! Good Mercutio!

ROMEO *tries to stop the fighting.* TYBALT *stabs* MERCUTIO *and then runs away with his companions*

MERCUTIO

I am hurt.
A plague o' both your houses! I am sped.
Is he gone, and hath nothing?

BENVOLIO

What, art thou hurt?

MERCUTIO

Ay, ay, a scratch, a scratch; marry, 'tis enough.
Where is my page? Go, villain, fetch a surgeon.

Exit Page

ROMEO

Courage, man; the hurt cannot be much.

MERCUTIO

No, 'tis not so deep as a well, nor so wide as a church door;
but 'tis enough, 'twill serve. Ask for me tomorrow, and you
shall find me a grave man. I am peppered, I warrant, for this
world. A plague o' both your houses! 'Zounds, a dog, a rat,
a mouse, a cat, to scratch a man to death! A braggart, a
rogue, a villain, that fights by the book of arithmetic! Why
the devil came you between us? I was hurt under your arm.

ROMEO

I thought all for the best.

MERCUTIO

Help me into some house, Benvolio,
Or I shall faint. A plague o' both your houses!
They have made worms' meat of me. I have it,
And soundly too. Your houses!

Exeunt MERCUTIO *and* BENVOLIO

ROMEO

This gentleman, the Prince's near ally,
My very friend, hath got this mortal hurt
In my behalf; my reputation stained

DISK LINK
Test your knowledge of the play in WALK-THROUGH ROMEO AND JULIET. This quiz will sort the swans from the crows!

With Tybalt's slander—Tybalt, that an hour
Hath been my cousin! O sweet Juliet,
Thy beauty hath made me effeminate
And in my temper softened valour's steel!

Re-enter BENVOLIO

BENVOLIO
O Romeo, Romeo, brave Mercutio is dead!
That gallant spirit hath aspired the clouds,
Which too untimely here did scorn the earth.
ROMEO
This day's black fate on more days doth depend;
This but begins the woe others must end.

Re-enter TYBALT

BENVOLIO
Here comes the furious Tybalt back again.
ROMEO
Alive, in triumph! And Mercutio slain!
Away to heaven, respective lenity,
And fire-eyed fury be my conduct now!
Now, Tybalt, take the "villain" back again
That late thou gavest me; for Mercutio's soul
Is but a little way above our heads,
Staying for thine to keep him company.
Either thou, or I, or both, must go with him.
TYBALT
Thou, wretched boy, that didst consort him here,
Shalt with him hence.
ROMEO
(*Drawing his sword*) This shall determine that.

They fight; TYBALT *dies*

BENVOLIO
Romeo, away, be gone!
The citizens are up, and Tybalt slain.
Stand not amazed. The Prince will doom thee death
If thou art taken; hence, be gone, away!
ROMEO
O, I am fortune's fool!

BENVOLIO
Why dost thou stay?

Exit ROMEO

Enter CITIZENS

FIRST CITIZEN
  Which way ran he that killed Mercutio?
  Tybalt, that murderer, which way ran he?
BENVOLIO
  There lies that Tybalt.
FIRST CITIZEN
Up, Sir, go with me;
  I charge thee in the Prince's name, obey.

Enter PRINCE, attended; MONTAGUE, CAPULET, their Wives, and others

PRINCE
  Where are the vile beginners of this fray?
BENVOLIO
  O noble Prince, I can discover all
  The unlucky manage of this fatal brawl.
  There lies the man, slain by young Romeo,
  That slew thy kinsman, brave Mercutio.
LADY CAPULET
  Tybalt, my cousin! O my brother's child!
  O Prince! O cousin! Husband! O, the blood is spilled
  Of my dear kinsman! Prince, as thou art true,
  For blood of ours, shed blood of Montague.
  O cousin, cousin!
PRINCE
  Benvolio, who began this bloody fray?
BENVOLIO
  Tybalt, here slain, whom Romeo's hand did slay.
  Romeo, that spoke him fair, bade him bethink
  How nice the quarrel was, and urged withal
  Your high displeasure. All this utterèd
  With gentle breath, calm look, knees humbly bowed,
  Could not take truce with the unruly spleen
  Of Tybalt, deaf to peace, but that he tilts
  With piercing steel at bold Mercutio's breast,
  Who, all as hot, turns deadly point to point,
  And, with a martial scorn, with one hand beats
  Cold death aside, and with the other sends

It back to Tybalt, whose dexterity
Retorts it. Romeo he cries aloud,
"Hold, friends! friends, part!" and, swifter than his tongue,
His agile arm beats down their fatal points,
And 'twixt them rushes; underneath whose arm
An envious thrust from Tybalt hit the life
Of stout Mercutio, and then Tybalt fled;
But by and by comes back to Romeo,
Who had but newly entertained revenge,
And to't they go like lightning, for, ere I
Could draw to part them, was stout Tybalt slain,
And, as he fell, did Romeo turn and fly.
This is the truth, or let Benvolio die.

LADY CAPULET
He is a kinsman to the Montague;
Affection makes him false; he speaks not true.
Some twenty of them fought in this black strife,
And all those twenty could but kill one life.
I beg for justice, which thou, Prince, must give.
Romeo slew Tybalt, Romeo must not live.

PRINCE
Romeo slew him, he slew Mercutio.
Who now the price of his dear blood doth owe?

MONTAGUE
Not Romeo, Prince, he was Mercutio's friend;
His fault concludes but what the law should end,
The life of Tybalt.

PRINCE
                    And for that offence
Immediately we do exile him hence.
I have an interest in your hate's proceeding,
My blood for your rude brawls doth lie a-bleeding;
But I'll amerce you with so strong a fine
That you shall all repent the loss of mine.
I will be deaf to pleading and excuses;
Nor tears nor prayers shall purchase out abuses.
Therefore use none. Let Romeo hence in haste,
Else, when he's found, that hour is his last.
Bear hence this body and attend our will.
Mercy but murders, pardoning those that kill.

Exeunt

ACT 3 SCENE 2
NURSE TELLS JULIET ABOUT ROMEO'S
BANISHMENT AND JULIET HAS MIXED
EMOTIONS. SHE LOVES ROMEO AND
MOURNS TYBALT'S DEATH. SHE DEFENDS
ROMEO'S CHARACTER AGAINST NURSE'S
CRITICISM, AND NURSE PROMISES TO
BRING HIM TO HER ROOM THAT NIGHT.

SCENE 2

Juliet's bedroom

Enter JULIET

JULIET

    Gallop apace, you fiery-footed steeds,
    Towards Phoebus' lodging! Such a waggoner
    As Phaeton would whip you to the west,
    And bring in cloudy night immediately.
    Spread thy close curtain, love-performing night,
    That runaway's eyes may wink and Romeo
    Leap to these arms, untalked of and unseen.
    Lovers can see to do their amorous rites
    By their own beauties; or, if love be blind,
    It best agrees with night. Come, civil night,
    Thou sober-suited matron, all in black,
    And learn me how to lose a winning match,
    Played for a pair of stainless maidenhoods.
    Hood my unmanned blood, bating in my cheeks,
    With thy black mantle; till strange love, grown bold,
    Think true love acted simple modesty.
    Come, night; come, Romeo; come, thou day in night;
    For thou wilt lie upon the wings of night
    Whiter than new snow upon a raven's back.
    Come, gentle night; come, loving, black-browed night,
    Give me my Romeo; and, when he shall die,
    Take him and cut him out in little stars,
    And he will make the face of heaven so fine
    That all the world will be in love with night
    And pay no worship to the garish sun.
    O, I have bought the mansion of a love,
    But not possessed it; and, though I am sold,
    Not yet enjoyed. So tedious is this day
    As is the night before some festival
    To an impatient child that hath new robes
    And may not wear them. O, here comes my Nurse,

Enter NURSE, *with a rope ladder*

    And she brings news; and every tongue that speaks
    But Romeo's name speaks heavenly eloquence.
    Now, Nurse, what news? What hast thou there? The cords

That Romeo bid thee fetch?

NURSE

                                        Ay, ay, the cords.

She throws the ladder down

JULIET

Ay me! What news? Why dost thou wring thy hands?

NURSE

Ah, well-a-day! He's dead, he's dead, he's dead!
We are undone, lady, we are undone!
Alack the day! He's gone, he's killed, he's dead!

JULIET

Can heaven be so envious?

NURSE

                                Romeo can,
Though heaven cannot. O Romeo, Romeo!
Whoever would have thought it? Romeo!

JULIET

What devil art thou, that dost torment me thus?
This torture should be roared in dismal hell.
Hath Romeo slain himself? Say thou but "Ay,"
And that bare vowel "I" shall poison more
Than the death-darting eye of cockatrice.
I am not I, if there be such an "I;"
Or those eyes shut, that makes thee answer "Ay."
If he be slain, say "Ay;" or if not, "No."
Brief sounds determine of my weal or woe.

NURSE

I saw the wound, I saw it with mine eyes—
God save the mark!—here on his manly breast.
A piteous corse, a bloody piteous corse;
Pale, pale as ashes, all bedaubed in blood,
All in gore blood; I swounded at the sight.

JULIET

O, break, my heart! Poor bankrupt, break at once!
To prison, eyes, ne'er look on liberty!
Vile earth, to earth resign; end motion here;
And thou and Romeo press one heavy bier!

NURSE

O Tybalt, Tybalt, the best friend I had!
O courteous Tybalt, honest gentleman!
That ever I should live to see thee dead!

JULIET

What storm is this that blows so contrary?
Is Romeo slaughtered, and is Tybalt dead?
My dearest cousin, and my dearer lord?
Then, dreadful trumpet, sound the general doom!
For who is living if those two are gone?

NURSE

Tybalt is gone, and Romeo banishèd;
Romeo that killed him, he is banishèd.

JULIET

O God! Did Romeo's hand shed Tybalt's blood?

NURSE

It did, it did! Alas the day, it did!

JULIET

O serpent heart, hid with a flowering face!
Did ever dragon keep so fair a cave?
Beautiful tyrant! Fiend angelical!
Dove-feathered raven! Wolvish-ravening lamb!
Despisèd substance of divinest show!
Just opposite to what thou justly seem'st,
A damnèd saint, an honourable villain!
O nature, what hadst thou to do in hell,
When thou didst bower the spirit of a fiend
In moral paradise of such sweet flesh?
Was ever book containing such vile matter
So fairly bound? O that deceit should dwell
In such a gorgeous palace!

NURSE

There's no trust,
No faith, no honesty in men; all perjured,
All forsworn, all naught, all dissemblers.
Ah, where's my man? Give me some aqua vitae.
These griefs, these woes, these sorrows make me old.
Shame come to Romeo!

JULIET

Blistered be thy tongue
For such a wish! He was not born to shame.
Upon his brow shame is ashamed to sit;
For 'tis a throne where honour may be crowned
Sole monarch of the universal earth.
O, what a beast was I to chide at him!

NURSE

Will you speak well of him that killed your cousin?

JULIET

Shall I speak ill of him that is my husband?
Ah, poor my lord, what tongue shall smooth thy name,
When I, thy three-hours' wife, have mangled it?
But, wherefore, villain, didst thou kill my cousin?
That villain cousin would have killed my husband.
Back, foolish tears, back to your native spring;
Your tributary drops belong to woe,
Which you, mistaking, offer up to joy.
My husband lives, that Tybalt would have slain;
And Tybalt's dead, that would have slain my husband.
All this is comfort; wherefore weep I then?
Some word there was, worser than Tybalt's death,
That murdered me. I would forget it fain;
But, O, it presses to my memory,
Like damnèd guilty deeds to sinners' minds!
"Tybalt is dead, and Romeo—banishèd."
That "banishèd," that one word "banishèd,"
Hath slain ten thousand Tybalts. Tybalt's death
Was woe enough, if it had ended there;
Or, if sour woe delights in fellowship
And needly will be ranked with other griefs,
Why followed not, when she said, "Tybalt's dead,"
"Thy father," or "thy mother," nay, or both,
Which modern lamentations might have moved?
But with a rearward following Tybalt's death,
"Romeo is banishèd," to speak that word
Is father, mother, Tybalt, Romeo, Juliet,
All slain, all dead. "Romeo is banishèd!"
There is no end, no limit, measure, bound,
In that word's death; no words can that woe sound.
Where is my father and my mother, Nurse?

NURSE

Weeping and wailing over Tybalt's corse.
Will you go to them? I will bring you thither.

JULIET

Wash they his wounds with tears? Mine shall be spent,
When theirs are dry, for Romeo's banishment.
Take up those cords. Poor ropes, you are beguiled,
Both you and I, for Romeo is exiled.
He made you for a highway to my bed;
But I, a maid, die maiden-widowèd.
Come, cords, come, Nurse; I'll to my wedding bed;
And death, not Romeo, take my maidenhead!

DISK LINK
There's a quotation on this page that will help you play WHO SAID WHAT?

NURSE

Hie to your chamber. I'll find Romeo
To comfort you. I wot well where he is.
Hark ye, your Romeo will be here at night.
I'll to him; he is hid at Lawrence's cell.

JULIET

O, find him! Give this ring to my true knight,
And bid him come to take his last farewell.

Exeunt

ACT 3 SCENE 3

FRIAR LAWRENCE TELLS ROMEO THAT THE PRINCE HAS BANISHED HIM FROM VERONA. ROMEO IS DEVASTATED THAT HE CANNOT BE WITH JULIET, AND FRIAR LAWRENCE TRIES TO COMFORT HIM. NURSE ARRIVES AND TELLS HIM HOW UPSET JULIET IS. ROMEO TRIES TO STAB HIMSELF, BUT NURSE GRABS THE DAGGER. FRIAR LAWRENCE IS ANGRY AT THIS ATTEMPTED SUICIDE. HE REMINDS ROMEO THAT HE COULD HAVE BEEN SENTENCED TO DEATH, AND BEGINS TO PLAN HOW HE MAY BE BROUGHT BACK FROM EXILE.

SCENE 3
Friar Lawrence's cell

Enter FRIAR LAWRENCE

FRIAR LAWRENCE

Romeo, come forth; come forth, thou fearful man.
Affliction is enamoured of thy parts,
And thou art wedded to calamity.

Enter ROMEO

ROMEO

Father, what news? What is the Prince's doom?
What sorrow craves acquaintance at my hand,
That I yet know not?

FRIAR LAWRENCE

              Too familiar
Is my dear son with such sour company.
I bring thee tidings of the Prince's doom.

ROMEO

What less than doomsday is the Prince's doom?

FRIAR LAWRENCE

A gentler judgement vanished from his lips:
Not body's death, but body's banishment.

ROMEO

Ha, banishment! Be merciful, say "death;"
For exile hath more terror in his look,
Much more than death. Do not say "banishment."

FRIAR LAWRENCE

Hence from Verona art thou banishèd.
Be patient, for the world is broad and wide.

ROMEO
There is no world without Verona walls,
But purgatory, torture, hell itself.
Hence "banishèd" is banished from the world,
And world's exile is death. Then "banishèd,"
Is death mistermed. Calling death "banishèd,"
Thou cutt'st my head off with a golden axe,
And smilest upon the stroke that murders me.

FRIAR LAWRENCE
O deadly sin! O rude unthankfulness!
Thy fault our law calls death; but the kind Prince,
Taking thy part, hath rushed aside the law,
And turned that black word "death" to "banishment."
This is dear mercy, and thou seest it not.

ROMEO
'Tis torture, and not mercy. Heaven is here,
Where Juliet lives; and every cat and dog
And little mouse, every unworthy thing,
Live here in heaven and may look on her,
But Romeo may not. More validity,
More honourable state, more courtship lives
In carrion-flies than Romeo. They my seize
On the white wonder of dear Juliet's hand
And steal immortal blessing from her lips,
Who even in pure and vestal modesty
Still blush, as thinking their own kisses sin,
But Romeo may not; he is banishèd.
Flies may do this, but I from this must fly;
They are free men, but I am banishèd.
And say'st thou yet that exile is not death?
Hadst thou no poison mixed, no sharp-ground knife,
No sudden mean of death, though ne'er so mean,
But "banishèd" to kill me?—"banishèd?"
O Friar, the damnèd use that word in hell;
Howling attends it. How hast thou the heart,
Being a divine, a ghostly confessor,
A sin-absolver, and my friend professed,
To mangle me with that word "banishèd?"

FRIAR LAWRENCE
Thou fond madman, hear me a little speak.

ROMEO
O, thou wilt speak again of banishment.

FRIAR LAWRENCE
I'll give thee armour to keep off that word;

Adversity's sweet milk, philosophy,
To comfort thee, though thou art banishèd.

ROMEO

Yet "banishèd?" Hang up philosophy!
Unless philosophy can make a Juliet,
Displant a town, reverse a Prince's doom,
It helps not, it prevails not. Talk no more.

FRIAR LAWRENCE

O, then I see that madmen have no ears.

ROMEO

How should they, when that wise men have no eyes?

FRIAR LAWRENCE

Let me dispute with thee of thy estate.

ROMEO

Thou canst not speak of that thou dost not feel.
Wert thou as young as I, Juliet thy love,
An hour but married, Tybalt murderèd,
Doting like me and like me banishèd,
Then mightst thou speak, then mightst thou tear thy hair,
And fall upon the ground, as I do now,
Taking the measure of an unmade grave.

ROMEO *throws himself to the floor. Knocking within*

FRIAR LAWRENCE

Arise; one knocks. Good Romeo, hide thyself.

ROMEO

Not I; unless the breath of heartsick groans,
Mist-like, infold me from the search of eyes.

Knocking

FRIAR LAWRENCE

Hark, how they knock! Who's there? Romeo, arise;
Thou wilt be taken. (*Calling*) Stay awhile! (*To* ROMEO)
    Stand up;

Knocking

Run to my study. (*Calling*) By and by! (*To* ROMEO) God's will,
What simpleness is this! (*Calling*) I come, I come!

Knocking

Who knocks so hard? Whence come you?
    What's your will?

NURSE

  (*From outside*) Let me come in, and you shall know
    my errand;
  I come from Lady Juliet.

FRIAR LAWRENCE

                 Welcome, then.

Enter NURSE

NURSE

  O holy Friar, O, tell me, holy Friar,
  Where is my lady's lord, where's Romeo?

FRIAR LAWRENCE

  There on the ground, with his own tears made drunk.

NURSE

  O, he is even in my mistress' case,
  Just in her case! O woeful sympathy!
  Piteous predicament! Even so lies she,
  Blubbering and weeping, weeping and blubbering.
  (*To* ROMEO) Stand up, stand up; stand, and you be a man.
  For Juliet's sake, for her sake, rise and stand!
  Why should you fall into so deep an O?

ROMEO

  Nurse!

NURSE

        Ah Sir! Ah Sir! Death's the end of all.

ROMEO

  Spak'st thou of Juliet? How is it with her?
  Doth she not think me an old murderer,
  Now I have stained the childhood of our joy
  With blood removed but little from her own?
  Where is she? And how doth she? And what says
  My concealed lady to our cancelled love?

NURSE

  O, she says nothing, Sir, but weeps and weeps;
  And now falls on her bed; and then starts up,
  And Tybalt calls, and then on Romeo cries,
  And then down falls again.

ROMEO

               As if that name,
  Shot from the deadly level of a gun,
  Did murder her; as that name's cursèd hand

Murdered her kinsman. O, tell me, Friar, tell me,
In what vile part of this anatomy
Doth my name lodge? Tell me, that I may sack
The hateful mansion.

He draws his dagger to kill himself; NURSE *grabs it from him*

FRIAR LAWRENCE
                          Hold thy desperate hand.
Art thou a man? Thy form cries out thou art;
Thy tears are womanish; thy wild acts denote
The unreasonable fury of a beast.
Unseemly woman in a seeming man!
And ill-beseeming beast in seeming both!
Thou hast amazed me. By my holy order,
I thought thy disposition better tempered.
Hast thou slain Tybalt? Wilt thou slay thyself?
And slay thy lady that in thy life lives,
By doing damnèd hate upon thyself?
Why rail'st thou on thy birth, the heaven, and earth?
Since birth, and heaven, and earth, all three do meet
In thee at once, which thou at once wouldst lose.
Fie, fie, thou shamest thy shape, thy love, thy wit,
Which, like a usurer, abound'st in all,
And usest none in that true use indeed
Which should bedeck thy shape, thy love, thy wit.
Thy noble shape is but a form of wax,
Digressing from the valour of a man;
Thy dear love sworn but hollow perjury,
Killing that love which thou hast vowed to cherish;
Thy wit, that ornament to shape and love,
Misshapen in the conduct of them both,
Like powder in a skilless soldier's flask,
Is set afire by thine own ignorance,
And thou dismembered with thine own defence.
What, rouse thee, man! Thy Juliet is alive,
For whose dear sake thou wast but lately dead.
There art thou happy. Tybalt would kill thee,
But thou slew'st Tybalt; there are thou happy.
The law that threatened death becomes thy friend
And turns it to exile; there art thou happy too.
A pack of blessings lights up upon thy back;
Happiness courts thee in her best array;
But, like a misbehaved and sullen wench,

Thou frown'st upon thy fortune and thy love.
Take heed, take heed, for such die miserable.
Go, get thee to thy love, as was decreed,
Ascend her chamber, hence and comfort her.
But look thou stay not till the watch be set,
For then thou canst not pass to Mantua,
Where thou shalt live, till we can find a time
To blaze your marriage, reconcile your friends,
Beg pardon of the Prince, and call thee back
With twenty hundred thousand times more joy
Than thou went'st forth in lamentation.
Go before, Nurse. Commend me to thy lady,
And bid her hasten all the house to bed,
Which heavy sorrow makes them apt unto.
Romeo is coming.

NURSE

O Lord, I could have stayed here all the night
To hear good counsel. O, what learning is!
My lord, I'll tell my lady you will come.

ROMEO

Do so, and bid my sweet prepare to chide.

NURSE

Here, Sir, a ring she bid me give you, Sir.
Hie you, make haste, for it grows very late.

Exit NURSE

ROMEO

How well my comfort is revived by this!

FRIAR LAWRENCE

Go hence; good night. And here stands all your state:
Either be gone before the watch be set,
Or by the break of day disguised from hence.
Sojourn in Mantua; I'll find out your man,
And he shall signify from time to time
Every good hap to you that chances here.
Give me thy hand. 'Tis late. Farewell; good night.

ROMEO

But that a joy past joy calls out on me,
It were a grief so brief to part with thee.
Farewell.

Exeunt

DISK LINK
Will Romeo make it to
Juliet's loving embrace? Answer
questions on the play and help
him climb to her balcony in
GIVE HER A KISS!

ACT 3 SCENE 4

CAPULET TELLS PARIS THAT HE CAN MARRY JULIET. HE BELIEVES THAT HIS DAUGHTER WILL DO ANYTHING HE ASKS OF HER, AND PLANS THE WEDDING FOR THREE DAYS' TIME.

SCENE 4
A room in Capulet's house

Enter CAPULET, LADY CAPULET, PARIS, *and a Servant*

CAPULET
Things have fallen out, Sir, so unluckily,
That we have had no time to move our daughter.
Look you, she loved her kinsman Tybalt dearly,
And so did I. Well, we were born to die.
'Tis very late, she'll not come down tonight.
I promise you, but for your company,
I would have been a-bed an hour ago.

PARIS
These times of woe afford no time to woo.
Madam, good night. Commend me to your daughter.

LADY CAPULET
I will, and know her mind early tomorrow;
Tonight she's mewed up to her heaviness.

CAPULET
Sir Paris, I will make a desperate tender
Of my child's love. I think she will be ruled
In all respects by me—nay, more, I doubt it not.
Wife, go you to her ere you go to bed;
Acquaint her here of my son Paris' love;
And bid her, mark you me, on Wednesday next—
But, soft! What day is this?

PARIS
                                    Monday, my lord,

CAPULET
Monday! Ha, ha! Well, Wednesday is too soon,
O' Thursday let it be. O' Thursday, tell her,
She shall be married to this noble earl.
Will you be ready? Do you like this haste?
We'll keep no great ado—a friend or two;
For, hark you, Tybalt being slain so late,
It may be thought we held him carelessly,
Being our kinsman, if we revel much.
Therefore we'll have some half a dozen friends,
And there an end. But what say you to Thursday?

PARIS
My lord, I would that Thursday were tomorrow.

CAPULET

> Well get you gone. O' Thursday be it then.
> Go you to Juliet ere you go to bed;
> Prepare her, wife, against this wedding day.
> Farewell, my lord. (*To a Servant*) Light to my chamber, ho!
> Afore me! It is so very very late, that we
> May call it early by and by. Good night.

Exeunt

ACT 3 SCENE 5

AFTER SPENDING THE NIGHT TOGETHER, ROMEO AND JULIET WAKE UP AT DAWN. NURSE WARNS THEM THAT JULIET'S MOTHER IS ON HER WAY, AND THAT ROMEO MUST LEAVE. LADY CAPULET TELLS HER DAUGHTER THAT HER FATHER HAS PLANNED HER WEDDING. JULIET IS HORRIFIED AND REFUSES TO MARRY PARIS. WHEN CAPULET HEARS THIS, HE IS FURIOUS AND THREATENS TO DISOWN HER. JULIET DECIDES TO GO TO FRIAR LAWRENCE TO SEEK ADVICE.

DISK LINK

Can you remember all the characters, props, and sound effects in this scene? Test yourself in MAKE A SCENE.

SCENE 5
Juliet's bedroom

ROMEO *and* JULIET *stand at a window*

JULIET

> Wilt thou be gone? It is not yet near day.
> It was the nightingale, and not the lark,
> That pierced the fearful hollow of thine ear.
> Nightly she sings on yond pomegranate tree.
> Believe me, love, it was the nightingale.

ROMEO

> It was the lark, the herald of the morn,
> No nightingale. Look, love, what envious streaks
> Do lace the severing clouds in yonder east.
> Night's candles are burnt out, and jocund day
> Stands tiptoe on the misty mountain tops.
> I must be gone and live, or stay and die.

JULIET

> Yond light is not daylight, I know it, I.
> It is some meteor that the sun exhales,
> To be to thee this night a torchbearer,
> And light thee on thy way to Mantua.
> Therefore stay yet; thou need'st not to be gone.

ROMEO

> Let me be ta'en, let me be put to death.
> I am content, so thou wilt have it so.
> I'll say yond grey is not the morning's eye,
> 'Tis but the pale reflex of Cynthia's brow;
> Nor that is not the lark, whose notes do beat
> The vaulty heaven so high above our heads.
> I have more care to stay than will to go.

Come, death, and welcome! Juliet wills it so.
How is't, my soul? Let's talk; it is not day.

JULIET

It is, it is! Hie hence, be gone, away!
It is the lark that sings so out of tune,
Straining harsh discords and unpleasing sharps.
Some say the lark makes sweet division;
This doth not so, for she divideth us.
Some say the lark and loathèd toad change eyes,
O, now I would they had changed voices too,
Since arm from arm that voice doth us affray,
Hunting thee hence with hunt's-up to the day.
O, now be gone; more light and light it grows.

ROMEO

More light and light; more dark and dark our woes!

Enter NURSE

NURSE

Madam!

JULIET

Nurse?

NURSE

Your lady mother is coming to your chamber:
The day is broke; be wary, look about.

Exit NURSE

JULIET

Then, window, let day in, and let life out.

ROMEO

Farewell, farewell! One kiss, and I'll descend.

He climbs down the ladder

JULIET

Art thou gone so? Love, lord, ay, husband, friend!
I must hear from thee every day in the hour,
For in a minute there are many days.
O, by this count I shall be much in years
Ere I again behold my Romeo!

ROMEO

(*From the orchard below*) Farewell!
I will omit no opportunity
That may convey my greetings, love, to thee.

JULIET
O think'st thou we shall ever meet again?

ROMEO
I doubt it not; and all these woes shall serve
For sweet discourses in our time to come.

JULIET
O God, I have an ill-divining soul!
Methinks I see thee, now thou art so low,
As one dead in the bottom of a tomb.
Either my eyesight fails, or thou look'st pale.

ROMEO
And trust me, love, in my eye so do you.
Dry sorrow drinks our blood. Adieu, adieu!

Exit

JULIET
O fortune, fortune! All men call thee fickle.
If thou art fickle, what dost thou with him
That is renowned for faith? Be fickle, fortune;
For then, I hope, thou wilt not keep him long,
But send him back.

LADY CAPULET
(*Outside the door*) Ho, daughter! Are you up?

JULIET
Who is't that calls? It is my lady mother!
Is she not down so late, or up so early?
What unaccustomed cause procures her hither?

Enter LADY CAPULET

LADY CAPULET
Why, how now, Juliet?

JULIET
                        Madam, I am not well.

LADY CAPULET
Evermore weeping for your cousin's death?
What, wilt thou wash him from his grave with tears?
And if thou couldst, thou couldst not make him live;
Therefore, have done. Some grief shows much of love;
But much of grief shows still some want of wit.

JULIET
Yet let me weep for such a feeling loss.

LADY CAPULET
So shall you feel the loss, but not the friend

Which you weep for.

JULIET

                  Feeling so the loss,
I cannot choose but ever weep the friend.

LADY CAPULET

Well, girl, thou weep'st not so much for his death,
As that the villain lives which slaughtered him.

JULIET

What villain Madam?

LADY CAPULET

                 That same villain, Romeo.

JULIET

(*Aside*) Villain and he be many miles asunder.
(*To her mother*) God Pardon him! I do, with all my heart;
And yet no man like he doth grieve my heart.

LADY CAPULET

That is because the traitor murderer lives.

JULIET

Ay, Madam, from the reach of these my hands.
Would none but I might venge my cousin's death!

LADY CAPULET

We will have vengeance for it, fear thou not.
Then weep no more. I'll send to one in Mantua,
Where that same banished runagate doth live,
Shall give him such an unaccustomed dram,
That he shall soon keep Tybalt company;
And then, I hope, thou wilt be satisfied.

JULIET

Indeed, I never shall be satisfied
With Romeo, till I behold him—dead—
Is my poor heart so for a kinsman vexed.
Madam, if you could find out but a man
To bear a poison, I would temper it
That Romeo should, upon receipt thereof,
Soon sleep in quiet. O, how my heart abhors
To hear him named, and cannot come to him.
To wreak the love I bore my cousin
Upon his body that slaughtered him!

LADY CAPULET

Find thou the means, and I'll find such a man.
But now I'll tell thee joyful tidings, girl.

JULIET

And joy comes well in such a needy time.
What are they, I beseech your ladyship?

DISK LINK
Test your knowledge of the play in WALK-THROUGH ROMEO AND JULIET. This quiz will sort the swans from the crows!

LADY CAPULET

Well, well, thou hast a careful father, child;
One who, to put thee from thy heaviness,
Hath sorted out a sudden day of joy
That thou expect'st not, nor I looked not for.

JULIET

Madam, in happy time, what day is that?

LADY CAPULET

Marry, my child, early next Thursday morn,
The gallant, young and noble gentleman,
The County Paris, at Saint Peter's Church,
Shall happily make thee there a joyful bride.

JULIET

Now, by Saint Peter's Church and Peter too,
He shall not make me there a joyful bride.
I wonder at this haste, that I must wed
Ere he, that should be husband, comes to woo.
I pray you, tell my lord and father, Madam,
I will not marry yet; and, when I do, I swear,
It shall be Romeo, whom you know I hate,
Rather than Paris. These are news indeed!

LADY CAPULET

Here comes your father; tell him so yourself,
And see how he will take it at your hands.

Enter CAPULET *and* NURSE

CAPULET

When the sun sets, the air doth drizzle dew,
But for the sunset of my brother's son
It rains downright.
How now, a conduit, girl? What, still in tears?
Evermore showering? In one little body
Thou counterfeit'st a bark, a sea, a wind;
For still thy eyes, which I may call the sea,
Do ebb and flow with tears; the bark thy body is,
Sailing in this salt flood; the winds, thy sighs
Who, raging with thy tears, and they with them,
Without a sudden calm, will overset
Thy tempest-tossèd body. How now, wife!
Have you delivered to her our decree?

LADY CAPULET

Ay, Sir; but she will none, she gives you thanks.
I would the fool were married to her grave!

3.5

DISK LINK

There's a quotation on this page that will help you play WHO SAID WHAT?

CAPULET

Soft, take me with you, take me with you, wife.
How will she none? Doth she not give us thanks?
Is she not proud? Doth she not count her blest,
Unworthy as she is, that we have wrought
So worthy a gentleman to be her bride?

JULIET

Not proud you have; but thankful that you have.
Proud can I never be of what I hate,
But thankful even for hate, that is meant love.

CAPULET

How now, how now, chop-logic! What is this?
"Proud," and "I thank you," and "I thank you not;"
And yet "not proud," mistress minion, you,
Thank me no thankings, nor proud me no prouds,
But fettle your fine joints 'gainst Thursday next,
To go with Paris to Saint Peter's Church,
Or I will drag thee on a hurdle thither.
Out, you green-sickness carrion! Out, you baggage!
You tallow-face!

LADY CAPULET

(*To her husband*) Fie, fie! What, are you mad?

JULIET

Good father, I beseech you on my knees,
Hear me with patience but to speak a word.

CAPULET

Hang thee, young baggage! Disobedient wretch!
I tell thee what: get thee to church o' Thursday,
Or never after look me in the face!
Speak not, reply not, do not answer me;
My fingers itch. Wife, we scarce thought us blest
That God had lent us but this only child;
But now I see this one is one too much,
And that we have a curse in having her.
Out on her, hilding!

NURSE

                    God in heaven bless her!
You are to blame, my lord, to rate her so.

CAPULET

And why, my Lady Wisdom? Hold your tongue,
Good Prudence; smatter with your gossips, go.

NURSE

I speak no treason.

CAPULET

               O, God gi' good e'en.

NURSE

May not one speak?

CAPULET

Peace, you mumbling fool!
Utter your gravity o'er a gossip's bowl;
For here we need it not.

LADY CAPULET

                You are too hot.

CAPULET

God's bread! It makes me mad.
Day, night, hour, tide, time, work, play,
Alone, in company, still my care hath been
To have her matched; and having now provided
A gentleman of noble parentage,
Of fair demesnes, youthful, and nobly trained,
Stuffed, as they say, with honourable parts,
Proportioned as one's thought would wish a man—
And then to have a wretched puling fool,
A whining mammet, in her fortune's tender,
To answer, "I'll not wed; I cannot love,
I am too young; I pray you, pardon me."
But, as you will not wed, I'll pardon you.
Graze where you will you shall not house with me.
Look to't, think on't, I do not use to jest.
Thursday is near; lay hand on heart, advise.
And you be mine, I'll give you to my friend;
And you be not, hang, beg, starve, die in the streets,
For, by my soul, I'll ne'er acknowledge thee,
Nor what is mine shall never do thee good.
Trust to't, bethink you; I'll not be forsworn.

Exit

JULIET

Is there no pity sitting in the clouds,
That sees into the bottom of my grief?
O, sweet my mother, cast me not away!
Delay this marriage for a month, a week;
Or, if you do not, make the bridal bed
In that dim monument where Tybalt lies.

LADY CAPULET

Talk not to me, for I'll not speak a word.
Do as thou wilt, for I have done with thee.

Exit

JULIET

    O God! O Nurse, how shall this be prevented?
    My husband is on earth, my faith in heaven.
    How shall that faith return again to earth,
    Unless that husband send it me from heaven
    By leaving earth? Comfort me, counsel me.
    Alack, alack, that heaven should practise stratagems
    Upon so soft a subject as myself!
    What say'st thou? Hast thou not a word of joy?
    Some comfort, Nurse.

NURSE

                        Faith, here it is. Romeo
    Is banished; and all the world to nothing,
    That he dares ne'er come back to challenge you;
    Or, if he do, it needs must be by stealth.
    Then, since the case so stands as now it doth,
    I think it best you married with the County.
    O, he's a lovely gentleman!
    Romeo's a dishclout to him. An eagle, Madam,
    Hath not so green, so quick, so fair an eye
    As Paris hath. Beshrew my very heart,
    I think you are happy in this second match,
    For it excels your first; or if it did not,
    Your first is dead—or 'twere as good he were,
    As living here and you no use of him.

JULIET

    Speakest thou from thy heart?

NURSE

                              And from my soul too;
    Or else beshrew them both.

JULIET

    Amen!

NURSE

    What?

JULIET

    Well, thou hast comforted me marvellous much.
    Go in and tell my lady I am gone,
    Having displeased my father, to Lawrence's cell,
    To make confession and to be absolved.

NURSE

    Marry, I will; and this is wisely done.

Exit

JULIET
Ancient damnation! O most wicked fiend!
Is it more sin to wish me thus forsworn,
Or to dispraise my lord with that same tongue
Which she hath praised him with above compare
So many thousand times? Go, counsellor;
Thou and my bosom henceforth shall be twain.
I'll to the Friar, to know his remedy.
If all else fail, myself have power to die.

Exit

ACT 4

SCENE 1
Friar Lawrence's cell

ACT 4 SCENE 1
THE FRIAR UNDERSTANDS JULIET'S
ANGUISH AND, SINCE SHE SAYS SHE IS
WILLING TO COMMIT SUICIDE TO AVOID
MARRIAGE WITH PARIS, HE DECIDES THAT
SHE WILL BE BRAVE ENOUGH TO TRY HIS
PLAN. SHE WILL TAKE A POTION THAT
WILL MAKE HER SEEM TO BE DEAD. HER
FUNERAL WILL TAKE PLACE AND SHE WILL
BE PLACED IN THE FAMILY VAULT. FRIAR
LAWRENCE WILL ARRANGE FOR ROMEO
TO COME BACK AND BRING HER OUT
OF THE VAULT WHEN SHE AWAKENS.

DISK LINK
Can you remember all the
characters, props, and sound
effects in this scene? Test
yourself in MAKE A SCENE.

Enter FRIAR LAWRENCE *and* PARIS

FRIAR LAWRENCE
On Thursday, Sir? The time is very short.
PARIS
My father Capulet will have it so;
And I am nothing slow to slack his haste.
FRIAR LAWRENCE
You say you do not know the lady's mind?
Uneven is the course, I like it not.
PARIS
Immoderately she weeps for Tybalt's death,
And therefore have I little talked of love;
For Venus smiles not in a house of tears.
Now, Sir, her father counts it dangerous
That she doth give her sorrow so much sway,
And in his wisdom hastes our marriage,
To stop the inundation of her tears,
Which, too much minded by herself alone,
May be put from her by society.
Now do you know the reason of this haste.
FRIAR LAWRENCE
(*Aside*) I would I knew not why it should
                    be slowed.
Look, Sir, here comes the lady toward my cell.

Enter JULIET

PARIS
Happily met, my lady and my wife!
JULIET
That may be, Sir, when I may be a wife.
PARIS
That "may be" must be, love, on Thursday next.
JULIET
What must be shall be.
FRIAR LAWRENCE
                    That's a certain text.
PARIS
Come you to make confession to this father?

JULIET
To answer that, I should confess to you.

PARIS
Do not deny to him that you love me.

JULIET
I will confess to you that I love him.

PARIS
So will ye, I am sure, that you love me.

JULIET
If I do so, it will be of more price,
Being spoke behind your back, than to your face.

PARIS
Poor soul, thy face is much abused with tears.

JULIET
The tears have got small victory by that,
For it was bad enough before their spite.

PARIS
Thou wrong'st it, more than tears, with that report.

JULIET
That is no slander, Sir, which is a truth;
And what I spake, I spake it to my face.

PARIS
Thy face is mine, and thou hast slandered it.

JULIET
It may be so, for it is not mine own.
Are you at leisure, holy father, now;
Or shall I come to you at evening Mass?

FRIAR LAWRENCE
My leisure serves me, pensive daughter, now.
My lord, we must entreat the time alone.

PARIS
God shield I should disturb devotion!
Juliet, on Thursday early will I rouse ye.
Till then, adieu; and keep this holy kiss.

He kisses her and leaves

JULIET
O shut the door! And when thou hast done so,
Come weep with me; past hope, past cure,
    past help!

FRIAR LAWRENCE
Ah, Juliet, I already know thy grief;
It strains me past the compass of my wits.

I hear thou must, and nothing may prorogue it,
On Thursday next be married to this County.

JULIET

Tell me not, Friar, that thou hearest of this,
Unless thou tell me how I may prevent it.
If, in thy wisdom, thou canst give no help,
Do thou but call my resolution wise,
And with this knife I'll help it presently.
God joined my heart and Romeo's, thou our hands;
And ere this hand, by thee to Romeo sealed,
Shall be the label to another deed,
Or my true heart with treacherous revolt
Turn to another, this shall slay them both.
Therefore, out of thy long-experienced time,
Give me some present counsel, or, behold,
'Twixt my extremes and me this bloody knife
Shall play the umpire, arbitrating that
Which the commission of thy years and art
Could to no issue of true honour bring.
Be not so long to speak; I long to die,
If what thou speak'st speak not of remedy.

FRIAR LAWRENCE

Hold, daughter. I do spy a kind of hope,
Which craves as desperate an execution
As that is desperate which we would prevent.
If, rather than to marry County Paris,
Thou hast the strength of will to slay thyself,
Then is it likely thou wilt undertake
A thing like death to chide away this shame,
That cop'st with death himself to scape from it;
And, if thou darest, I'll give thee remedy.

JULIET

O, bid me leap, rather than marry Paris,
From off the battlements of any tower;
Or walk in thievish ways; or bid me lurk
Where serpents are; chain me with roaring bears;
Or hide me nightly in a charnel-house,
O'er-covered quite with dead men's rattling bones,
With reeky shanks and yellow chapless skulls;
Or bid me go into a new-made grave
And hide me with a dead man in his shroud—
Things that, to hear them told, have made me tremble—
And I will do it without fear or doubt,
To live an unstained wife to my sweet love.

DISK LINK
There's a quotation on this page that will help you play WHO SAID WHAT?

FRIAR LAWRENCE

Hold, then; go home, be merry, give consent
To marry Paris. Wednesday is tomorrow.
Tomorrow night look that thou lie alone;
Let not thy Nurse lie with thee in thy chamber.
Take thou this vial, being then in bed,
And this distillèd liquor drink thou off;
When presently through all thy veins shall run
A cold and drowsy humour, for no pulse
Shall keep his native progress, but surcease.
No warmth, no breath, shall testify thou livest;
The roses in thy lips and cheeks shall fade
To wanny ashes, thy eyes' windows fall,
Like death, when he shuts up the day of life;
Each part, deprived of supple government,
Shall, stiff and stark and cold, appear like death;
And in this borrowed likeness of shrunk death
Thou shalt continue two and forty hours,
And then awake as from a pleasant sleep.
Now, when the bridegroom in the morning comes
To rouse thee from thy bed, there art thou dead.
Then, as the manner of our country is,
In thy best robes uncovered on the bier
Thou shalt be borne to that same ancient vault
Where all the kindred of the Capulets lie.
In the meantime, against thou shalt awake,
Shall Romeo by my letters know our drift,
And hither shall he come; and he and I
Will watch thy waking, and that very night
Shall Romeo bear thee hence to Mantua.
And this shall free thee from this present shame,
If no inconstant toy, nor womanish fear,
Abate thy valour in the acting it.

JULIET

Give me, give me! O, tell not me of fear!

FRIAR LAWRENCE

Hold; get you gone, be strong and prosperous
In this resolve. I'll send a friar with speed
To Mantua, with my letters to thy lord.

JULIET

Love give me strength! And strength shall help afford.
Farewell, dear father!

Exeunt

4.2

ACT 4 SCENE 2

JULIET RETURNS FROM FRIAR LAWRENCE'S CELL. SHE SAYS THAT SHE WAS WRONG TO REFUSE HER FATHER'S WISHES AND THAT SHE WILL GO THROUGH WITH THE MARRIAGE. CAPULET RESCHEDULES HER WEDDING FOR THE FOLLOWING DAY. JULIET AND NURSE GO TO CHOOSE JULIET'S WEDDING CLOTHES.

SCENE 2

A hall in Capulet's house

Enter CAPULET, LADY CAPULET, NURSE, *and two* SERVANTS

CAPULET
(*Giving a list to a* SERVANT) So many guests invite as here
are writ.

Exit FIRST SERVANT

(*To another* SERVANT) Sirrah, go hire me twenty cunning
cooks.
SECOND SERVANT
You shall have none ill, Sir; for I'll try if they
can lick their fingers.
CAPULET
How canst thou try them so?
SECOND SERVANT
Marry, Sir, 'tis an ill cook that cannot lick his
own fingers. Therefore he that cannot lick his own
fingers goes not with me.
CAPULET
Go, be gone.

Exit SECOND SERVANT

We shall be much unfurnished for this time.
What, is my daughter gone to Friar Lawrence?
NURSE
Ay, forsooth.
CAPULET
Well, he may chance to do some good on her.
A peevish self-willed harlotry it is.
NURSE
See where she comes from shrift with merry look.

Enter JULIET

CAPULET
How now, my headstrong! Where have you been gadding?
JULIET
Where I have learned me to repent the sin
Of disobedient opposition
To you and your behests, and am enjoined

By holy Lawrence to fall prostrate here,
And beg your pardon. Pardon, I beseech you!
Henceforward I am ever ruled by you.

CAPULET

Send for the County. Go tell him of this.
I'll have this knot knit up tomorrow morning.

JULIET

I met the youthful lord at Lawrence's cell,
And gave him what becomèd love I might,
Not stepping o'er the bounds of modesty.

CAPULET

Why, I am glad on't; this is well. Stand up.
This is as't should be. Let me see the County.
Ay, marry, go, I say, and fetch him hither.
Now, afore God, this reverend holy Friar,
All our whole city is much bound to him.

JULIET

Nurse, will you go with me into my closet,
To help me sort such needful ornaments
As you think fit to furnish me tomorrow?

LADY CAPULET

No, not till Thursday; there is time enough.

CAPULET

Go, Nurse, go with her. We'll to church tomorrow.

Exeunt JULIET *and* NURSE

LADY CAPULET

We shall be short in our provision.
'Tis now near night.

CAPULET

                                    Tush, I will stir about,
And all things shall be well, I warrant thee, wife.
Go thou to Juliet, help to deck up her.
I'll not to bed tonight. Let me alone.
I'll play the housewife for this once. (*He calls the* SERVANTS)
        What, ho!
They are all forth. Well, I will walk myself
To County Paris, to prepare up him
Against tomorrow. My heart is wondrous light,
Since this same wayward girl is so reclaimed.

Exeunt

ACT 4 SCENE 3

ASKING NURSE TO LEAVE HER ALONE FOR THE NIGHT, JULIET PREPARES TO DRINK THE DRUG THAT THE FRIAR HAS GIVEN HER. SHE IS WORRIED THAT IT MAY NOT WORK, THAT THE FRIAR MAY HAVE GIVEN HER A FATAL POISON, OR THAT SHE WILL WAKE UP IN THE TOMB BEFORE ROMEO ARRIVES. FINALLY, HOWEVER, SHE GATHERS HER COURAGE AND DRINKS THE POTION.

SCENE 3

Juliet's bedroom

Enter JULIET *and* NURSE

JULIET
    Ay, those attires are best; but, gentle Nurse,
    I pray thee, leave me to myself tonight,
    For I have need of many orisons
    To move the heavens to smile upon my state,
    Which, well thou know'st, is cross, and full of sin.

Enter LADY CAPULET

LADY CAPULET
    What, are you busy, ho? Need you my help?
JULIET
    No, madam; we have culled such necessaries
    As are behoveful for our state tomorrow.
    So please you, let me now be left alone,
    And let the Nurse this night sit up with you;
    For, I am sure, you have your hands full all
    In this so sudden business.
LADY CAPULET
                            Good night.
    Get thee to bed, and rest; for thou hast need.

Exeunt LADY CAPULET *and* NURSE

JULIET
    Farewell! God knows when we shall meet again.
    I have a faint cold fear thrills through my veins,
    That almost freezes up the heat of life.
    I'll call them back again to comfort me.
    Nurse!—What should she do here?
    My dismal scene I needs must act alone.
    Come, vial.
    What if this mixture do not work at all?
    Shall I be married then tomorrow morning?
    No, no. This shall forbid it. Lie thou there.

Laying down her dagger

What if it be a poison, which the Friar
Subtly hath ministered to have me dead,
Lest in this marriage he should be dishonoured,
Because he married me before to Romeo?
I fear it is; and yet, methinks, it should not,
For he hath still been tried a holy man.
How if, when I am laid into the tomb,
I wake before the time that Romeo
Come to redeem me? There's a fearful point!
Shall I not, then, be stifled in the vault,
To whose foul mouth no healthsome air breathes in,
And there die strangled ere my Romeo comes?
Or, if I live, is it not very like,
The horrible conceit of death and night,
Together with the terror of the place—
As in a vault, an ancient receptacle,
Where, for these many hundred years, the bones
Of all my buried ancestors are packed;
Where bloody Tybalt, yet but green in earth,
Lies festering in his shroud; where, as they say,
At some hours in the night spirits resort—
Alack, alack, is it not like that I,
So early waking, what with loathsome smells,
And shrieks like mandrakes torn out of the earth,
That living mortals, hearing them, run mad:
O, if I wake, shall I not be distraught,
Environed with all these hideous fears,
And madly play with my forefather's joints,
And pluck the mangled Tybalt from his shroud?
And, in this rage, with some great kinsman's bone,
As with a club, dash out my desperate brains?
O, look! Methinks I see my cousin's ghost
Seeking out Romeo, that did spit his body
Upon a rapier's point. Stay, Tybalt, stay!
Romeo, I come! This do I drink to thee.

She falls upon her bed, within the curtains

ACT 4 SCENE 4
PREPARATIONS ARE BEING MADE FOR
THE WEDDING FEAST. PARIS HAS ARRIVED
TO ESCORT JULIET TO THE CHURCH,
BUT SHE IS NOT YET AWAKE. NURSE
IS SENT TO WAKE JULIET.

SCENE 4

A hall in Capulet's house

Enter LADY CAPULET *and* NURSE

LADY CAPULET
Hold, take these keys, and fetch more spices, Nurse.

NURSE
They call for dates and quinces in the pastry.

Enter CAPULET

CAPULET
Come, stir, stir, stir! The second cock hath crowed,
The curfew bell hath rung, 'tis three o'clock.
Look to the baked meats, good Angelica;
Spare not for cost.

NURSE
                              Go, you cot-quean, go,
Get you to bed! Faith, you'll be sick tomorrow
For this night's watching.

CAPULET
No, not a whit. What! I have watched ere now
All night for lesser cause, and ne'er been sick.

LADY CAPULET
Ay, you have been a mouse-hunt in your time;
But I will watch you from such watching now.

Exeunt LADY CAPULET *and* NURSE

CAPULET
A jealous hood, a jealous hood!

Enter SERVANTS, *with spits, logs, and baskets*

                              Now, fellow, What is there?

FIRST SERVANT
Things for the cook, Sir, but I know not what.

CAPULET
Make haste, make haste.

Exit FIRST SERVANT

(*To* SECOND SERVANT) Sirrah, fetch drier logs.

Call Peter, he will show thee where they are.

SECOND SERVANT
I have a head, Sir, that will find out logs,
And never trouble Peter for the matter.

Exit

CAPULET
Mass, and well said; a merry whoreson, ha!
Thou shalt be loggerhead. Good faith, 'tis day.
The County will be here with music straight,
For so he said he would. (*Music sounds*) I hear him near.
Nurse! Wife! What, ho! What, Nurse, I say!

Re-enter NURSE

Go waken Juliet, go and trim her up.
I'll go and chat with Paris. Hie, make haste,
Make haste! the bridegroom he is come already:
Make haste, I say.

Exeunt

ACT 4 SCENE 5
NURSE FINDS JULIET APPARENTLY DEAD. EVERYONE IN THE HOUSE MOURNS JULIET'S DEATH. FRIAR LAWRENCE SCOLDS THEM FOR THEIR RECENT TREATMENT OF HER, SAYING THAT JULIET IS BETTER OFF IN HEAVEN. HE TELLS THEM TO PREPARE FOR HER FUNERAL.

SCENE 5
Juliet's bedroom

Enter NURSE

NURSE
Mistress! What, mistress! Juliet! Fast, I warrant her, she.
Why, lamb! Why, lady! Fie, you slug-a-bed!
Why, love, I say! Madam! Sweet-heart! Why, bride!
What, not a word? You take your pennyworths now;
Sleep for a week; for the next night, I warrant,
The County Paris hath set up his rest,
That you shall rest but little. God forgive me,
Marry, and amen, how sound is she asleep!
I needs must wake her. Madam, madam, madam!
Ay, let the County take you in your bed!
He'll fright you up, i' faith. Will it not be?

Undraws the bed curtains

107

4.5

DISK LINK
There are a couple of quotations on this page that will help you play WHO SAID WHAT?

What, dressed! And in your clothes, and down again!
I must needs wake you; Lady! lady! lady!
Alas, alas! Help, help! My lady's dead!
O, well-a-day, that ever I was born!
Some aqua vitae, ho! My lord! My lady!

Enter LADY CAPULET

LADY CAPULET
What noise is here?

NURSE
      O lamentable day!

LADY CAPULET
What is the matter?

NURSE
     Look, look! O heavy day!

LADY CAPULET
O me, O me! My child, my only life,
Revive, look up, or I will die with thee!
Help, help! Call help.

Enter CAPULET

CAPULET
For shame, bring Juliet forth; her lord is come.

NURSE
She's dead, deceased, she's dead; alack the day!

LADY CAPULET
Alack the day, she's dead, she's dead, she's dead!

CAPULET
Ha! let me see her. Out, alas! She's cold,
Her blood is settled, and her joints are stiff;
Life and these lips have long been separated.
Death lies on her like an untimely frost
Upon the sweetest flower of all the field.

NURSE
O lamentable day!

LADY CAPULET
O woeful time!

CAPULET
Death, that hath ta'en her hence to make me wail,
Ties up my tongue, and will not let me speak.

Enter FRIAR LAWRENCE *and* PARIS, *with* MUSICIANS

FRIAR LAWRENCE

Come, is the bride ready to go to church?

CAPULET

Ready to go, but never to return.
O son! The night before thy wedding day
Hath Death lain with thy wife. There she lies,
Flower as she was, deflowerèd by him.
Death is my son-in-law, Death is my heir;
My daughter he hath wedded. I will die,
And leave him all; life, living, all is Death's.

PARIS

Have I thought long to see this morning's face,
And doth it give me such a sight as this?

LADY CAPULET

Accursed, unhappy, wretched, hateful day!
Most miserable hour that e'er time saw
In lasting labour of his pilgrimage!
But one, poor one, one poor and loving child,
But one thing to rejoice and solace in,
And cruel Death hath catched it from my sight!

NURSE

O woe! O woeful, woeful, woeful day!
Most lamentable day, most woeful day,
That ever, ever, I did yet behold!
O day! O day! O day! O hateful day!
Never was seen so black a day as this.
O woeful day, O woeful day!

PARIS

Beguiled, divorcèd, wrongèd, spited, slain!
Most detestable Death, by thee beguiled,
By cruel cruel thee quite overthrown!
O love! O life! Not life, but love in death!

CAPULET

Despised, distressed, hated, martyred, killed!
Uncomfortable time, why camest thou now
To murder, murder our solemnity?
O child! O child! My soul, and not my child!
Dead art thou! Alack, my child is dead;
And with my child my joys are burièd.

FRIAR LAWRENCE

Peace, ho, for shame! Confusion's cure lives not
In these confusions. Heaven and yourself
Had part in this fair maid; now Heaven hath all,
And all the better is it for the maid.

Your part in her you could not keep from Death,
But heaven keeps his part in eternal life.
The most you sought was her promotion.
For 'twas your heaven she should be advanced;
And weep ye now, seeing she is advanced
Above the clouds, as high as heaven itself?
O, in this love, you love your child so ill,
That you run mad, seeing that she is well.
She's not well married that lives married long;
But she's best married that dies married young.
Dry up your tears, and stick your rosemary
On this fair corse; and, as the custom is,
In all her best array bear her to church;
For though fond nature bids us all lament,
Yet nature's tears are reason's merriment.

CAPULET
All things that we ordainèd festival,
Turn from their office to black funeral;
Our instruments to melancholy bells,
Our wedding cheer to a sad burial feast,
Our solemn hymns to sullen dirges change,
Our bridal flowers serve for a buried corse,
And all things change them to the contrary.

FRIAR LAWRENCE
Sir, go you in; and, Madam, go with him;
And go, Sir Paris. Everyone prepare
To follow this fair corse unto her grave.
The heavens do lour upon you for some ill;
Move them no more by crossing their high will.

Exeunt CAPULET, LADY CAPULET, PARIS, *and* FRIAR LAWRENCE

FIRST MUSICIAN
Faith, we may put up our pipes, and be gone.
NURSE
Honest good fellows, ah, put up, put up;
For, well you know, this is a pitiful case.
FIRST MUSICIAN
Ay, by my troth, the case may be amended.

Exit NURSE

Enter PETER

PETER
Musicians, O, musicians, "Heart's ease,
Heart's ease!" O, and you will have me live, play
"Heart's ease."

FIRST MUSICIAN
Why "Heart's ease?"

PETER
O, musicians, because my heart itself plays "My heart is full."
O, play me some merry dump, to comfort me.

FIRST MUSICIAN
Not a dump we; 'tis no time to play now.

PETER
You will not, then?

FIRST MUSICIAN
No.

PETER
I will then give it you soundly.

FIRST MUSICIAN
What will you give us?

PETER
No money, on my faith, but the gleek; I will give
you the minstrel.

FIRST MUSICIAN
Then will I give you the serving-creature.

PETER
Then will I lay the serving-creature's dagger on your pate. I
will carry no crotchets. I'll re you, I'll fa you; do you note me?

FIRST MUSICIAN
And you re us and fa us, you note us.

SECOND MUSICIAN
Pray you, put up your dagger, and put out your wit.

PETER
Then have at you with my wit! I will dry-beat you with an
iron wit, and put up my iron dagger.
Answer me like men:
    When griping grief the heart doth wound,
    And doleful dumps the mind oppress,
    Then music with her silver sound—
Why "silver sound?" Why "music with her silver sound?"
What say you, Simon Catling?

FIRST MUSICIAN
Marry, Sir, because silver hath a sweet sound.

PETER
Pretty! What say you, Hugh Rebeck?

SECOND MUSICIAN

I say "silver sound," because musicians sound for silver.

PETER

Pretty too! What say you, James Soundpost?

THIRD MUSICIAN

Faith, I know not what to say.

PETER

O, I cry you mercy! You are the singer. I will say for you. It is "music with her silver sound," because musicians have no gold for sounding.

Then music with her silver sound
With speedy help doth lend redress.

Exit PETER

FIRST MUSICIAN

What a pestilent knave is this same!

SECOND MUSICIAN

Hang him, Jack! Come, we'll in here; tarry for the mourners, and stay dinner.

Exeunt

ACT 5

SCENE 1
A street in Mantua

ACT 5 SCENE 1
HAVING DREAMED THAT SOMETHING GOOD WAS ABOUT TO HAPPEN, ROMEO, IN EXILE IN MANTUA, IS DEVASTATED BY BALTHASAR'S NEWS OF JULIET'S DEATH. HE DECIDES TO BUY SOME POISON AND KILL HIMSELF BESIDE HER IN THE TOMB.

Enter ROMEO

ROMEO
If I may trust the flattering truth of sleep,
My dreams presage some joyful news at hand.
My bosom's lord sits lightly in his throne,
And all this day an unaccustomed spirit
Lifts me above the ground with cheerful thoughts.
I dreamt my lady came and found me dead—
Strange dream, that gives a dead man leave to think!—
And breathed such life with kisses in my lips,
That I revived, and was an emperor.
Ah me! How sweet is love itself possessed,
When but love's shadows are so rich in joy!

Enter BALTHASAR

News from Verona!—How now, Balthasar?
Dost thou not bring me letters from the Friar?
How doth my lady? Is my father well?
How fares my Juliet? That I ask again,
For nothing can be ill, if she be well.

BALTHASAR
Then she is well, and nothing can be ill:
Her body sleeps in Capel's monument,
And her immortal part with angels lives.
I saw her laid low in her kindred's vault,
And presently took post to tell it you.
O, pardon me for bringing these ill news,
Since you did leave it for my office, Sir.

ROMEO
Is it even so? Then I defy you, stars!
Thou know'st my lodging. Get me ink and paper,
And hire post-horses. I will hence tonight.

BALTHASAR
I do beseech you, Sir, have patience.
Your looks are pale and wild, and do import
Some misadventure.

ROMEO
                    Tush, thou art deceived.

Leave me, and do the thing I bid thee do.
Hast thou no letters to me from the Friar?

BALTHASAR

No, my good lord.

ROMEO

No matter. Get thee gone,
And hire those horses. I'll be with thee straight.

Exit BALTHASAR

Well, Juliet, I will lie with thee tonight.
Let's see for means. O mischief, thou art swift
To enter in the thoughts of desperate men!
I do remember an apothecary,
And hereabouts he dwells, which late I noted
In tattered weeds, with overwhelming brows,
Culling of simples. Meagre were his looks,
Sharp misery had worn him to the bones;
And in his needy shop a tortoise hung,
An alligator stuffed, and other skins
Of ill-shaped fishes; and about his shelves
A beggarly account of empty boxes,
Green earthen pots, bladders and musty seeds,
Remnants of packthread and old cakes of roses,
Were thinly scattered, to make up a show.
Noting this penury, to myself I said:
"And if a man did need a poison now,
Whose sale is present death in Mantua,
Here lives a caitiff wretch would sell it him."
O, this same thought did but forerun my need,
And this same needy man must sell it me.
As I remember, this should be the house.
Being holiday, the beggar's shop is shut.
What, ho! Apothecary!

Enter APOTHECARY

APOTHECARY

Who calls so loud?

ROMEO

Come hither, man. I see that thou art poor.
Hold, there is forty ducats. Let me have
A dram of poison, such soon-speeding gear
As will disperse itself through all the veins

That the life-weary taker may fall dead,
And that the trunk may be discharged of breath
As violently as hasty powder fired
Doth hurry from the fatal cannon's womb.

APOTHECARY
Such mortal drugs I have; but Mantua's law
Is death to any he that utters them.

ROMEO
Art thou so bare and full of wretchedness,
And fear'st to die? Famine is in thy cheeks,
Need and oppression starveth in thine eyes,
Contempt and beggary hangs upon thy back;
The world is not thy friend nor the world's law;
The world affords no law to make thee rich;
Then be not poor, but break it, and take this.

APOTHECARY
My poverty, but not my will, consents.

ROMEO
I pay thy poverty, and not thy will.

APOTHECARY
Put this in any liquid thing you will,
And drink it off; and, if you had the strength
Of twenty men, it would dispatch you straight.

ROMEO
There is thy gold—worse poison to men's souls,
Doing more murder in this loathsome world,
Than these poor compounds that thou mayst not sell.
I sell thee poison; thou hast sold me none.
Farewell. Buy food, and get thyself in flesh.
Come, cordial and not poison, go with me
To Juliet's grave; for there must I use thee.

Exeunt

ACT 5 SCENE 2
FRIAR LAWRENCE DISCOVERS THAT
THE LETTER HE WROTE TO ROMEO
OUTLINING HIS PLAN WAS NEVER SENT.
HE HAD ENTRUSTED IT TO FRIAR JOHN,
WHO HAD LATER BEEN LOCKED UP IN A
HOUSE SUSPECTED OF HARBORING THE
PLAGUE. WITH JULIET ABOUT TO WAKE
UP, FRIAR LAWRENCE HURRIES OFF TO
THE VAULT HIMSELF.

SCENE 2
Friar Lawrence's cell

Enter FRIAR JOHN

FRIAR JOHN
Holy Franciscan! Friar! Brother, ho!

Enter FRIAR LAWRENCE

FRIAR LAWRENCE
This same should be the voice of Friar John.
Welcome from Mantua. What says Romeo?
Or, if his mind be writ, give me his letter.

FRIAR JOHN
Going to find a barefoot brother out,
One of our order, to associate me,
Here in this city visiting the sick,
And finding him, the searchers of the town,
Suspecting that we both were in a house
Where the infectious pestilence did reign,
Sealed up the doors, and would not let us forth;
So that my speed to Mantua there was stayed.

FRIAR LAWRENCE
Who bore my letter, then, to Romeo?

FRIAR JOHN
I could not send it—here it is again—
Nor get a messenger to bring it thee,
So fearful were they of infection.

FRIAR LAWRENCE
Unhappy fortune! By my brotherhood,
The letter was not nice, but full of charge
Of dear import, and the neglecting it
May do much danger. Friar John, go hence;
Get me an iron crow, and bring it straight
Unto my cell.

FRIAR JOHN
Brother, I'll go and bring it thee.

Exit

FRIAR LAWRENCE
Now must I to the monument alone;
Within this three hours will fair Juliet wake.
She will beshrew me much that Romeo
Hath had no notice of these accidents;
But I will write again to Mantua,
And keep her at my cell till Romeo come;
Poor living corse, closed in a dead man's tomb!

Exit

ACT 5 SCENE 3

PARIS VISITS JULIET'S TOMB TO SAY PRAYERS FOR HER, BUT HEARS SOME FOOTSTEPS AND HIDES. WHEN ROMEO TRIES TO FORCE OPEN THE VAULT, PARIS CONFRONTS HIM AND THEY FIGHT. PARIS IS KILLED. ROMEO FINDS JULIET'S BODY AND DRINKS THE POISON HE HAS BROUGHT WITH HIM. FRIAR LAWRENCE ARRIVES TOO LATE, AND JULIET WAKES TO FIND ROMEO DEAD BY HER SIDE. SHE KILLS HERSELF WITH HIS DAGGER. THE TWO FAMILIES ARRIVE ON THE SCENE, AND FRIAR LAWRENCE EXPLAINS WHAT HAS HAPPENED. MONTAGUE AND CAPULET VOW TO END THEIR FEUD.

DISK LINK
Can you remember all the characters, props, and sound effects in this scene? Test yourself in MAKE A SCENE.

SCENE 3

In a churchyard, outside a tomb belonging to the Capulets

Enter PARIS, *and his* PAGE *bearing flowers and a torch*

PARIS
Give me thy torch, boy. Hence, and stand aloof.
Yet put it out, for I would not be seen.
Under yond yew trees lay thee all along,
Holding thine ear close to the hollow ground,
So shall no foot upon the churchyard tread,
Being loose, unfirm with digging up of graves,
But thou shalt hear it. Whistle then to me,
As signal that thou hear'st something approach.
Give me those flowers. Do as I bid thee, go.

PAGE
(*Aside*) I am almost afraid to stand alone
Here in the churchyard; yet I will adventure.

He hides behind the trees

PARIS
Sweet flower, with flowers thy bridal bed I strew—
O woe, thy canopy is dust and stones—
Which with sweet water nightly I will dew,
Or, wanting that, with tears distilled by moans.
The obsequies that I for thee will keep
Nightly shall be to strew thy grave and weep.

The PAGE *whistles*

The boy gives warning something doth approach.
What cursèd foot wanders this way tonight,
To cross my obsequies and true love's rite?
What, with a torch! Muffle me, night, awhile.

He hides

Enter ROMEO *and* BALTHASAR, *with a torch, mattock, and a crowbar*

ROMEO
Give me that mattock and the wrenching iron.

DISK LINK
Guess what Shakespeare's more difficult words and phrases mean in the GLOSSARY GAME.

Hold, take this letter; early in the morning
See thou deliver it to my lord and father.
Give me the light. Upon thy life, I charge thee,
Whate'er thou hear'st or seest, stand all aloof,
And do not interrupt me in my course.
Why I descend into this bed of death
Is partly to behold my lady's face;
But chiefly to take thence from her dead finger
A precious ring, a ring that I must use
In dear employment. Therefore hence, be gone.
But if thou, jealous, dost return to pry
In what I farther shall intend to do,
By heaven, I will tear thee joint by joint
And strew this hungry churchyard with thy limbs.
The time and my intents are savage-wild,
More fierce and more inexorable far
Than empty tigers or the roaring sea.

BALTHASAR
I will be gone, Sir, and not trouble you.

ROMEO
So shalt thou show me friendship. (*Gives him money*)
     Take thou that.
Live, and be prosperous; and farewell, good fellow.

BALTHASAR
(*Aside*) For all this same, I'll hide me hereabout.
His looks I fear, and his intents I doubt.

He hides nearby

ROMEO
(*Forcing the tomb open*) Thou detestable maw, thou
     womb of death,
Gorged with the dearest morsel of the earth,
Thus I enforce thy rotten jaws to open,
And, in despite, I'll cram thee with more food!

PARIS
This is that banished haughty Montague,
That murdered my love's cousin, with which grief,
It is supposed, the fair creature died;
And here is come to do some villainous shame
To the dead bodies. I will apprehend him.
(*Comes forward*) Stop thy unhallowed toil, vile
     Montague!
Can vengeance be pursued further than death?

Condemnèd villain, I do apprehend thee.
Obey, and go with me; for thou must die.

ROMEO

I must indeed; and therefore came I hither.
Good gentle youth, tempt not a desperate man.
Fly hence, and leave me. Think upon these gone;
Let them affright thee. I beseech thee, youth,
Put not another sin upon my head
By urging me to fury. O, be gone!
By heaven, I love thee better than myself;
For I come hither armed against myself.
Stay not, be gone. Live, and hereafter say,
A madman's mercy bade thee run away.

PARIS

I do defy thy conjurations,
And apprehend thee for a felon here.

ROMEO

Wilt thou provoke me? Then have at thee, boy!

They fight

PAGE

O Lord, they fight! I will go call the watch.

Exit

PARIS

(*Falls*) O, I am slain! If thou be merciful,
Open the tomb, lay me with Juliet.

Dies

ROMEO

In faith, I will. Let me peruse this face.
Mercutio's kinsman, noble County Paris!
What said my man when my betossèd soul,
Did not attend him as we rode? I think
He told me Paris should have married Juliet.
Said he not so? Or did I dream it so?
Or am I mad, hearing him talk of Juliet,
To think it was so? O, give me thy hand,
One writ with me in sour misfortune's book!
I'll bury thee in a triumphant grave.
A grave? O no, a lantern, slaughtered youth,
For here lies Juliet, and her beauty makes

This vault a feasting presence full of light.
Death, lie thou there, by a dead man interred.

He lays PARIS *in the tomb*

How oft when men are at the point of death
Have they been merry, which their keepers call
A lightning before death! O, how may I
Call this a lightning? O my love! My wife!
Death, that hath sucked the honey of thy breath,
Hath had no power yet upon thy beauty.
Thou art not conquered. Beauty's ensign yet
Is crimson in thy lips and in thy cheeks,
And death's pale flag is not advancèd there.
Tybalt, liest thou there in thy bloody sheet?
O, what more favour can I do to thee,
Than with that hand that cut thy youth in twain
To sunder his that was thine enemy?
Forgive me, cousin! Ah, dear Juliet,
Why art thou yet so fair? Shall I believe
That unsubstantial Death is amorous,
And that the lean abhorrèd monster keeps
Thee here in dark to be his paramour?
For fear of that, I still will stay with thee;
And never from this palace of dim night
Depart again. Here, here will I remain
With worms that are thy chambermaids. O, here
Will I set up my everlasting rest,
And shake the yoke of inauspicious stars
From this world-wearied flesh. Eyes, look your last!
Arms, take your last embrace! And lips, O you
The doors of breath, seal with a righteous kiss
A dateless bargain to engrossing Death!
Come, bitter conduct, come, unsavoury guide!
Thou desperate pilot, now at once run on
The dashing rocks thy sea-sick weary bark!
Here's to my love! (*Drinks the poison*) O true apothecary!
Thy drugs are quick. Thus with a kiss I die.

Dies

Enter, at the other end of the churchyard, FRIAR LAWRENCE,
with a lantern, crowbar, and spade

FRIAR LAWRENCE

Saint Francis be my speed! How oft tonight
Have my old feet stumbled at graves! Who's there?

BALTHASAR

Here's one, a friend, and one that knows you well.

FRIAR LAWRENCE

Bliss be upon you! Tell me, good my friend,
What torch is yond, that vainly lends his light
To grubs and eyeless skulls? As I discern,
It burneth in the Capel's monument.

BALTHASAR

It doth so, holy Sir; and there's my master,
One that you love.

FRIAR LAWRENCE

Who is it?

BALTHASAR

Romeo.

FRIAR LAWRENCE

How long hath he been there?

BALTHASAR

Full half an hour.

FRIAR LAWRENCE

Go with me to the vault.

BALTHASAR

I dare not, Sir
My master knows not but I am gone hence;
And fearfully did menace me with death
If I did stay to look on his intents.

FRIAR LAWRENCE

Stay, then; I'll go alone. Fear comes upon me.
O, much I fear some ill unthrifty thing.

BALTHASAR

As I did sleep under this yew tree here,
I dreamt my master and another fought,
And that my master slew him.

FRIAR LAWRENCE

Romeo!
Alack, alack, what blood is this, which stains
The stony entrance of this sepulchre?
What mean these masterless and gory swords
To lie discoloured by this place of peace?

Enters the tomb

DISK LINK
There are a couple of quotations on this page that will help you play WHO SAID WHAT?

Romeo! O, pale! Who else? What, Paris too?
And steeped in blood? Ah, what an unkind hour
Is guilty of this lamentable chance!
The lady stirs!

JULIET wakes

JULIET

O comfortable Friar! Where is my lord?
I do remember well where I should be,
And there I am. Where is my Romeo?

Noise of WATCHMEN outside

FRIAR LAWRENCE

I hear some noise. Lady, come from that nest
Of death, contagion, and unnatural sleep.
A greater power than we can contradict
Hath thwarted our intents. Come, come away.
Thy husband in thy bosom there lies dead;
And Paris too. Come, I'll dispose of thee
Among a sisterhood of holy nuns.
Stay not to question, for the watch is coming.
Come, go, good Juliet. (*Noise again*) I dare no longer stay.

JULIET

Go, get thee hence, for I will not away.

Exit FRIAR LAWRENCE

What's here? A cup, closed in my true love's hand?
Poison, I see, hath been his timeless end.
O churl! Drunk all, and left no friendly drop
To help me after? I will kiss thy lips.
Haply some poison yet doth hang on them,
To make me die with a restorative.
(*Kisses him*) Thy lips are warm.

FIRST WATCHMAN

(*Outside*) Lead, boy. Which way?

JULIET

Yea, noise? Then I'll be brief. O happy dagger!

Snatching ROMEO'S dagger

This is thy sheath; (*Stabs herself*) there rust,
        and let me die.

Falls on ROMEO'S *body, and dies*

Enter WATCHMEN *and* PAGE *of* PARIS

PAGE
This is the place; there, where the torch doth burn.
FIRST WATCHMAN
The ground is bloody; search about the churchyard.
Go, some of you, whoe'er you find attach.

Exeunt some of the WATCHMEN

Pitiful sight! Here lies the County slain,
And Juliet bleeding, warm, and newly dead,
Who here hath lain these two days burièd.
Go, tell the Prince, run to the Capulets,
Raise up the Montagues; some others search.

Exeunt other WATCHMEN

We see the ground whereon these woes do lie;
But the true ground of all these piteous woes
We cannot without circumstance descry.

Re-enter a WATCHMAN, *with* BALTHASAR

SECOND WATCHMAN
Here's Romeo's man; we found him in the churchyard.
FIRST WATCHMAN
Hold him in safety, till the Prince come hither.

Re-enter other WATCHMEN, *with* FRIAR LAWRENCE

THIRD WATCHMAN
Here is a Friar that trembles, sighs and weeps.
We took this mattock and this spade from him,
As he was coming from this churchyard's side.
FIRST WATCHMAN
A great suspicion! Stay the Friar too.

Enter the PRINCE, *and Attendants*

PRINCE
What misadventure is so early up,
That calls our person from our morning rest?

Enter CAPULET, *and* LADY CAPULET, *and others*

CAPULET
What should it be, that they so shriek abroad?

LADY CAPULET
The people in the street cry "Romeo,"
Some "Juliet," and some "Paris;" and all run,
With open outcry toward our monument.

PRINCE
What fear is this which startles in our ears?

FIRST WATCHMAN
Sovereign, here lies the County Paris slain;
And Romeo dead; and Juliet, dead before,
Warm and new killed.

PRINCE
Search, seek, and know how this foul murder comes.

FIRST WATCHMAN
Here is a Friar, and slaughtered Romeo's man,
With instruments upon them, fit to open
These dead men's tombs.

CAPULET
O heavens! O wife, look how our daughter bleeds!
This dagger hath mista'en, for, lo, his house
Is empty on the back of Montague,
And it mis-sheathèd in my daughter's bosom!

LADY CAPULET
O me! This sight of death is as a bell,
That warns my old age to a sepulchre.

Enter MONTAGUE, *and others*

PRINCE
Come, Montague; for thou art early up,
To see thy son and heir more early down.

MONTAGUE
Alas, my liege, my wife is dead tonight!
Grief of my son's exile hath stopped her breath.
What further woe conspires against mine age?

PRINCE
Look, and thou shalt see.

MONTAGUE
(*Seeing* ROMEO) O thou untaught! What manners is in this?
To press before thy father to a grave?

PRINCE

    Seal up the mouth of outrage for a while,
    Till we can clear these ambiguities,
    And know their spring, their head, their true descent;
    And then will I be general of your woes,
    And lead you even to death. Meantime forbear,
    And let mischance be slave to patience.
    Bring forth the parties of suspicion.

FRIAR LAWRENCE

    I am the greatest, able to do least,
    Yet most suspected, as the time and place
    Doth make against me of this direful murder;
    And here I stand, both to impeach and purge
    Myself condemnèd and myself excused.

PRINCE

    Then say at once what thou dost know in this.

FRIAR LAWRENCE

    I will be brief, for my short date of breath
    Is not so long as is a tedious tale.
    Romeo, there dead, was husband to that Juliet;
    And she, there dead, that Romeo's faithful wife.
    I married them; and their stolen marriage day
    Was Tybalt's doomsday, whose untimely death
    Banished the new-made bridegroom from this city;
    For whom, and not for Tybalt, Juliet pined.
    You, to remove that siege of grief from her,
    Betrothed and would have married her perforce
    To County Paris. Then comes she to me,
    And, with wild looks, bid me devise some mean
    To rid her from this second marriage,
    Or in my cell there would she kill herself.
    Then gave I her, so tutored by my art,
    A sleeping potion; which so took effect
    As I intended, for it wrought on her
    The form of death. Meantime I writ to Romeo,
    That he should hither come as this dire night,
    To help to take her from her borrowed grave,
    Being the time the potion's force should cease.
    But he which bore my letter, Friar John,
    Was stayed by accident, and yesternight
    Returned my letter back. Then all alone
    At the prefixèd hour of her waking,
    Came I to take her from her kindred's vault;
    Meaning to keep her closely at my cell,

Till I conveniently could send to Romeo.
But when I came, some minute ere the time
Of her awakening, here untimely lay
The noble Paris and true Romeo dead.
She wakes; and I entreated her come forth,
And bear this work of heaven with patience,
But then a noise did scare me from the tomb;
And she, too desperate, would not go with me,
But, as it seems, did violence on herself.
All this I know; and to the marriage
Her Nurse is privy; and, if aught in this
Miscarried by my fault, let my old life
Be sacrificed, some hour before his time,
Unto the rigour of severest law.

PRINCE

We still have known thee for a holy man.
Where's Romeo's man? What can he say to this?

BALTHASAR

I brought my master news of Juliet's death;
And then in post he came from Mantua
To this same place, to this same monument.
This letter he early bid me give his father,
And threatened me with death, going in the vault,
I departed not and left him there.

PRINCE

Give me the letter; I will look on it.
Where is the County's page that raised the watch?

The PAGE comes forward

Sirrah, what made your master in this place?

PAGE

He came with flowers to strew his lady's grave,
And bid me stand aloof, and so I did.
Anon comes one with light to ope the tomb;
And by and by my master drew on him;
And then I ran away to call the watch.

PRINCE

This letter doth make good the Friar's words,
Their course of love, the tidings of her death;
And here he writes that he did buy a poison
Of a poor 'pothecary, and therewithal
Came to this vault to die, and lie with Juliet.
Where be these enemies? Capulet! Montague!

See, what a scourge is laid upon your hate,
That heaven finds means to kill your joys with love.
And I, for winking at your discords too,
Have lost a brace of kinsmen. All are punished.

CAPULET

O brother Montague, give me thy hand.
This is my daughter's jointure, for no more
Can I demand.

MONTAGUE

But I can give thee more;
For I will raise her statue in pure gold,
That whiles Verona by that name is known,
There shall no figure at such rate be set
As that of true and faithful Juliet.

CAPULET

As rich shall Romeo's by his lady's lie;
Poor sacrifices of our enmity!

PRINCE

A glooming peace this morning with it brings.
The sun, for sorrow, will not show his head.
Go hence, to have more talk of these sad things;
Some shall be pardoned, and some punishèd:
For never was a story of more woe
Than this of Juliet and her Romeo.

Exeunt

NOTES

NOTES

NOTES

NOTES

NOTES

NOTES

NOTES

NOTES

NOTES

NOTES

RUNNING YOUR INTERFACT SHAKESPEARE DISK

Your INTERFACT SHAKESPEARE CD-ROM will run both on PCs with Windows and on Apple Macintosh computers.

To make sure that your computer meets the system requirements, check the list below.

MINIMUM SYSTEM REQUIREMENTS

PC
◇ Pentium 166Mhz or faster processor
◇ Windows 95+PC
◇ 32Mb RAM
◇ 16-bit color display
◇ Soundcard
◇ 640 x 480 graphics

Apple Macintosh
◇ PowerMacs and above (200Mhz processor)
◇ System 8.1 (or later)
◇ 32Mb RAM
◇ Color monitor set to at least 640 x 480 graphics
◇ 16-bit color display

LOADING YOUR INTERFACT SHAKESPEARE DISK

INTERFACT SHAKESPEARE is easy to use. You can run INTERFACT SHAKESPEARE from the CD-ROM, so all you have to do is place it in the appropriate drive of your computer—you do not need to install the program on your hard drive. Before you begin, quickly run through the checklist below to ensure that your computer is ready to run INTERFACT SHAKESPEARE.

PC WITH WINDOWS

The program should start automatically when you put the disk in the CD-ROM drive. If it does not, follow these instructions:
1 Put the disk in the CD-ROM drive of your computer
2 Double-click MY COMPUTER
3 Double-click CD-ROM drive icon
4 Double-click on the ROMEO & JULIET icon to start

APPLE MACINTOSH

1 Put the disk in the CD-ROM drive of your computer
2 Double-click on the INTERFACT SHAKESPEARE icon
3 Double-click on the ROMEO & JULIET icon to start

CHECKLIST

◇ Firstly, make sure that your computer and monitor meet the system requirements on page 138.

◇ Make sure that your computer, monitor, and CD-ROM drive are all switched on and working properly.

◇ It is important that you don't have other applications running, such as word processors. Before starting INTERFACT SHAKESPEARE, quit all other applications.

◇ Make sure any screen savers for your computer have been switched off.

How to Use Interfact Shakespeare

INTERFACT SHAKESPEARE is easy
to use. First find out how to load the
program (see page 138) then read these
simple instructions and dive in!

There are seven different features to explore. Use the heart buttons at the bottom of the screen to select a feature or a game. You will see that the main area of the screen changes when you click on different features.

For example, this is what your screen will look like when you play MAKE A SCENE, a game where you try to remember some of the characters, props, and sound effects in certain scenes of the play. Each game comes with instructions and help text.

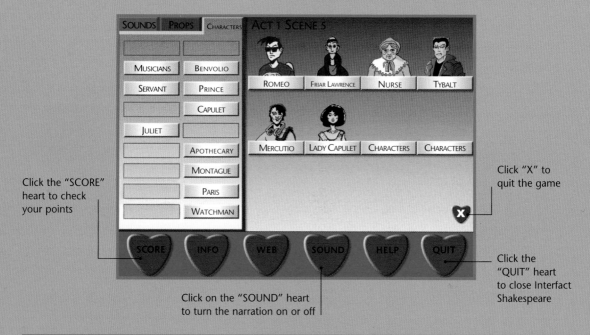

Click the "SCORE" heart to check your points

Click "X" to quit the game

Click the "QUIT" heart to close Interfact Shakespeare

Click on the "SOUND" heart to turn the narration on or off

DISK LINKS

When you read the play, you'll come across Disk Links. These show you where to find activities on the CD-ROM that relate to the page that you are reading. Watch for Disk Links as they will help you score more points when you play the games on the disk!

BOOKMARKS

As you use the games and features on the disk, you'll see Bookmarks. These give you page references in the book which will help you to play the games. Just turn to the page of the book shown in the Bookmark and you'll find the answer you need.

INFORMATION

For easy-to-access information about the play, click on the "INFO" heart on the main menu of the CD-ROM. The Time Line and Meet the Characters screens give an overview of who's who and the play's main events. For further information, click on our Web link.

DISK LINK

There's a quotation on this page that will help you to play WHO SAID WHAT.

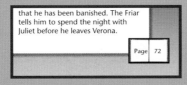

that he has been banished. The Friar tells him to spend the night with Juliet before he leaves Verona.

Page 72

HOT DISK TIPS

◇ If you need help finding your way around the disk, click on the "HELP" heart to go to the help section. This will give you information on how to access each feature, how to play the games, and scoring for the CD-ROM.

◇ Click on the main screen to move on at any time. Use the "QUIT" button to exit the CD-ROM and use the "X" button to close the game you are in, or to close a popup.

◇ Keep a close eye on the cursor. When it changes from an arrow to a hand, click your mouse and something will happen.

TROUBLESHOOTING

If you have a problem with your INTERFACT SHAKESPEARE CD-ROM, you should find the solution here. If you can't, first try contacting us for assistance by e-mail: helpline@two-canpublishing.com. If you do not get a response, call the telephone helpline on 609 921 6700. Leave a message and we will get back to you as soon as we can.

> Run through these general checkpoints before consulting Common Problems on the next page.

YOUR COMPUTER SETUP

Resetting the screen resolution in Windows 95 or 98: *QUICK TIPS*
Click on START at the bottom left of your screen, then click on SETTINGS, then CONTROL PANEL, then double-click on DISPLAY. Click on the SETTINGS tab at the top.

Reset the Desktop area (or Display area) to 640 x 480 pixels and choose 16-bit color display, then click APPLY.

You may need to restart your computer after changing display settings.

Adjusting the Virtual Memory in Windows 95 or 98: *QUICK TIPS*
It is not recommended that these settings are adjusted because Windows will automatically configure your system as required.

Adjusting the Virtual Memory on Apple Macintosh: *QUICK TIPS*
If you have 32Mb of RAM or more, ROMEO & JULIET will run faster. If you do not have this amount of RAM free, hard disk memory can be used by switching on Virtual Memory. Select the APPLE MENU, CONTROL PANELS, then select MEMORY. Switch on Virtual Memory. Set the amount of memory you require, then restart.

Disk will not run

There may not be enough memory available. Quit all other applications. If this does not work, increase your machine's RAM by adjusting the Virtual Memory (see page 142).

There is no sound
(Try each of the following)

1 Make sure that your speakers or headphones are connected to the speaker outlet at the back of your computer. Make sure they are not plugged into the audio socket next to the CD-ROM drive at the front of the computer.

2 Make sure the volume control is turned up (on your external speakers and by using internal volume control).

3 (PCs only) Your soundcard is not SoundBlaster compatible. To make your settings SoundBlaster compatible, see your soundcard manual for more information.

Graphics are missing or poor quality

Not enough memory is available or you have the wrong display setting. Either quit other applications and programs or make sure that your monitor control is set to 16-bit color display.

Graphics freeze or text boxes appear blank (Windows 95 or 98)

Graphics card acceleration is too high. Right-click your mouse on MY COMPUTER. Click on PROPERTIES, then PERFORMANCE, then GRAPHICS. Reset the hardware acceleration slider to "None." Click OK. Restart your computer.

Your machine freezes

There is not enough memory available. Either quit other applications and programs or increase your machine's RAM by adjusting the Virtual Memory (see page 142).

PRINCETON · LONDON